The Age of Global Change

The Age of Global Change

Culture, Power, and Identity

Hamid Yeganeh

The Age of Global Change: Culture, Power, and Identity

First published in 2026 by
Business Expert Press, LLC
222 East 46th Street, New York, NY 10017
www.businessexpertpress.com

ISBN-13: 978-1-63742-934-1 (paperback)
ISBN-13: 978-1-63742-935-8 (e-book)

Business Expert Press International Business Collection

First edition: 2026

10 9 8 7 6 5 4 3 2 1

EU SAFETY REPRESENTATIVE
Mare Nostrum Group B.V.
Mauritskade 21D
1091 GC Amsterdam
The Netherlands
gpsr@mare-nostrum.co.uk

Description

The Age of Global Change **provides an in-depth examination of the major forces reshaping societies in the twenty-first century, by referring to themes of demography, globalization, cultural change, inequality, governance, health, and sustainability.**

It highlights how rapid population growth, urbanization, migration, and shifts in religious and linguistic patterns are transforming the social fabric worldwide. At the same time, globalization has brought about profound cultural shifts, fostering individualism, gender equality, and diversity discourses, while also provoking nationalist and populist reactions.

This book discusses the emergence of a global culture defined by hyperconnectivity, symbolic consumption, and the post-truth condition, alongside the rise of contested phenomena such as wokeism that reflect deeper struggles over identity and values. In international affairs, the book situates these changes within a broader geopolitical realignment, where the decline of Western dominance is matched by the ascent of multipolar power centers, particularly in Asia. Economic inequality and corporate concentration of power are shown to exacerbate global divides, fueled by financialization, tax evasion, and crony capitalism. Health and sustainability are positioned as defining challenges of the century.

From pandemics to mental health crises, and from climate change to ecological degradation, these issues highlight the vulnerabilities and interdependencies of an interconnected world. The author argues that humanity is undergoing a paradoxical transformation, marked by both fragmentation and integration, the persistence of traditions amid modernization, and escalating risks accompanied by new possibilities. **Ultimately, the century will be shaped not only by crises but also by opportunities for innovation, cultural synthesis, and collective action.**

Contents

CHAPTER 1

Demography Is Destiny

An Incredible Growth of the Human Population

For thousands of years, human population growth remained extremely slow. Around 10,000 BCE, the world population was an estimated 2.4 million, reaching about 295 million by 1,000 CE. Even as recently as 200 years ago, Earth's population was still below 1 billion. This pattern changed dramatically in the 18th century. The Industrial Revolution, alongside advancements in medicine, agriculture, and sanitation, ignited a population boom. By the 1830s, the global population reached 1 billion, then doubled to 2 billion by the 1930s, and only 30 years later, it hit 3 billion in the 1960s [1]. Population growth accelerated from there, skyrocketing to 7 billion by 2011—a 133 percent increase in just 50 years (Table 1.1 and Figure 1.1). By late 2024, the world's population will have reached 8.2 billion. This figure reflects a significant increase from the 7.6 billion recorded in mid-2017, indicating a growth of about 600 million individuals over the past seven years [2].

This surge in growth rates, especially during the 1950s and 1960s, stemmed mainly from rapid declines in death rates across developing nations. The United Nations Population Division projects that the world's population will reach 9 billion by 2038, and exceed 10 billion by 2056 [1]. If these estimates hold, humanity will have grown by 7 billion people in the century from 1956 to 2056—an astonishing 234 percent increase. To visualize it, a global population of 10 billion would be equivalent to adding today's populations of China and India to our current world count.

The rapid population growth between the 1950s and 1970s strained many nations' development efforts, prompting the adoption of birth control and family planning programs. By the 1990s, growth rates had slowed, influenced by these programs and the spread of diseases like HIV/ AIDS. Today, the global population is growing more slowly than in the 1970s and 1980s.

Historically, three major phases of population growth have emerged. The first phase, before the 17th century, saw very slow growth due to limited resources and low life expectancy. The second phase began in the 18th century with modern advancements, marked by rising living standards and improved health. The third phase started in the 1980s, when growth rates, particularly in developed nations, began to decline.

While growth rates have slowed, the world's population will likely continue to rise in the short- and medium term. Fertility rates in developing countries remain high, and survival rates are improving, making further population growth by 2050 almost inevitable. Recent projections estimate that the global population will range between 8.4 and 8.6 billion by 2030 and between 9.5 and 13.3 billion by 2100.

In addition to global population growth, we should pay attention to the distribution, density, and uneven patterns of growth across the world, as these issues imply important consequences.

As of 2024, Asia's population is approximately 4.8 billion, constituting about 60 percent of the global population [3]. This significant proportion underscores Asia's status as the most populous continent, home to nearly three-fifths of all people worldwide. Following Asia, Africa's population is approximately 1.5 billion, accounting for about 18.3 percent of the global population. Europe has about 745 million (9.1%), and Latin America and the Caribbean together have approximately 663 million people (8.1%). North America and Oceania have smaller populations, with about 386 million (4.7%) and 46 million (0.6%), respectively. Notably, India and China are the two most populous countries globally, with populations of approximately 1.45 billion and 1.42 billion, respectively. Combined, these two nations comprise nearly 35.2 percent of the global population [4].

This distribution highlights a significant imbalance: low-income countries in Asia and Africa have the largest populations and highest population densities. At the same time, high-income regions such as Europe and North America are less densely populated. Additionally, many high-income countries have experienced low fertility rates and high life expectancies over the past seven decades [5]. In contrast, developing

Table 1.1 World population historical data

Year	Population	Yearly Change (%)	Yearly Change	Urban Population (%)	Urban Population
2023	8,029,898,732	1.11	88,153,373	54.7	4,392,354,606
2022	7,941,745,358	1.11	87,185,613	54.7	4,344,134,711
2021	7,854,559,745	1.11	86,228,477	54.7	4,296,444,181
2020	7,768,331,268	1.11	85,281,848	54.7	4,249,277,204
2015	7,349,472,099	1.18	83,949,411	53.80	3,957,285,013
2010	6,929,725,043	1.23	82,017,839	51.50	3,571,272,167
2005	6,519,635,850	1.25	78,602,746	49.10	3,199,013,076
2000	6,126,622,121	1.33	78,299,807	46.60	2,856,131,072
1995	5,735,123,084	1.55	85,091,077	44.80	2,568,062,984
1990	5,309,667,699	1.82	91,425,426	43	2,285,030,904
1985	4,852,540,569	1.79	82,581,621	41.30	2,003,049,795
1980	4,439,632,465	1.80	75,646,647	39.40	1,749,539,272
1975	4,061,399,228	1.98	75,782,307	37.80	1,534,721,238
1970	3,682,487,691	2.08	71,998,514	36.70	1,350,280,789
1965	3,322,495,121	1.94	60,830,259	N.A.	N.A.
1960	3,018,343,828	1.82	52,005,861	33.80	1,019,494,911
1955	2,758,314,525	1.78	46,633,043	N.A.	N.A.

HUMAN POPULATION GROWTH

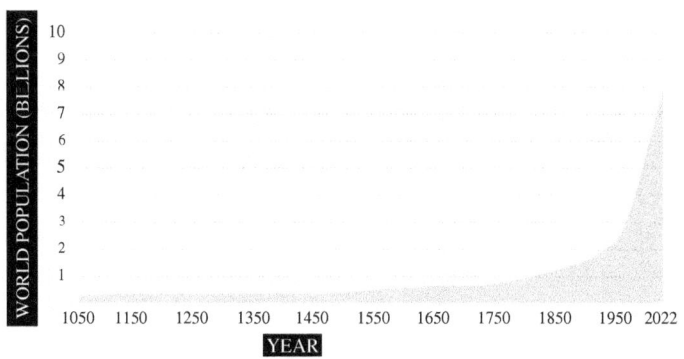

Figure 1.1 World population growth over time, 1050–2050

nations continue to exhibit high fertility rates alongside improving life expectancy and declining infant mortality. For instance, the least developed countries had an average fertility rate of about 4.3 children per woman between 2010 and 2015, with growth rates estimated at approximately 2.4 percent per year [6, 7].

Generally, population growth rates are inversely related to levels of socioeconomic development. The poorest and least developed regions, particularly sub-Saharan Africa and the Indian subcontinent, experience the highest population growth rates.

There is also a notable disparity in median age between wealthy and poorer nations. For example, in 2024, Europe had a median age of 42.5 years, making it the oldest continent. In contrast, many developing countries had median ages around 20 years. In 2024, 25 percent of Europe's population was aged 60 or over, compared to 12 percent in Latin America and the Caribbean, 13 percent in Asia, and only 6 percent in Africa [7].

The Diverging Growth Rates: Sub-Saharan Africa and India Are the Fastest-Growing Areas

The global population is expected to grow in the next five decades, but there are significant disparities across the world (Figure 1.2). Those countries with lower median age levels are poised to have the highest population growth in the coming years. As shown in Table 1.2, Africa has the highest population growth rate at 2.4 percent, while Europe has the lowest growth rate at _0.17 percent. This high rate of population growth in Africa means that the African population is expected to double in the next 28 years. Based on similar projections, more than half of the global population growth in the next four decades will occur in Africa. Between now and 2100, the populations of many African countries are expected to increase at least three- to fourfold. The populations of impoverished African countries such as Angola, Burundi, the Democratic Republic of the Congo, Malawi, Mali, Niger, Somalia, Uganda, the United Republic of Tanzania, and Zambia are projected to increase fivefold by 2100 [6]. Nigeria may surpass the United States to become the world's third populous country by 2050.

Simply put, 1.3 billion people will be added only in Africa between now and 2050, while Asia, mainly India, is responsible for an increase of another billion people for the same period [8]. Based on similar forecasts, the drastic population growth in Africa, unlike Asia, will continue even

World population by region, 1950 to 2100
Projected population to 2100 is based on the UN's medium population scenario.

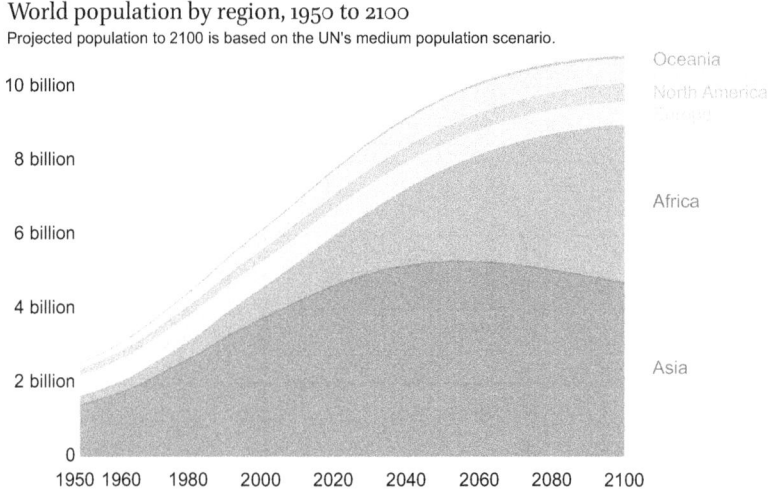

Figure 1.2 Population growth by region, 1950–2100

after 2050 [6]. Consequently, sub-Saharan Africa's share of the global population is projected to grow to 25 percent by 2050 and 39 percent by 2100, while the share of the people residing in Asia will fall to 54 percent by 2050 and 44 percent by 2100.

As of 2023, India has surpassed China to become the world's most populous country, with an estimated population of approximately 1.428 billion, accounting for about 18 percent of the global population. China's population stands at approximately 1.425 billion, also representing about 18 percent of the world's total. These two nations are on divergent demographic trajectories. Unlike China, the fertility rate in India has remained very high (Table 1.3). India's population is projected to reach 1.5 billion in 2030 and 1.7 billion in 2050, whereas China's population is expected to remain relatively stable until the 2030s, followed by a slight decline [6]. Northern America, Latin America, and the Caribbean, and Oceania are projected to experience smaller population growth levels, while Europe is expected to have a population decline by 2050. By 2050, the populations in six countries could exceed 300 million, including China, India, Indonesia, Nigeria, Pakistan, and the United States. The population growth in the following decades will be so uneven that nine countries will be responsible for more than half of the world's population

Table 1.2 *Distribution of the world's population by region*

Region	Population (2023)	Yearly Change (%)	Net Change	Migrants (Net)	Fertility Rate	Median Age	Urban Population (%)	World Share (%)
Asia	4,753,079,727	0.64	30,444,963	-1,487,191	1.93	32	52.6	59.1
Africa	1,460,481,772	2.37	33,745,467	-535,151	4.18	19	44.7	18.2
Europe	742,272,652	-0.17	-1,283,113	792,167	1.5	42	75.7	9.2
Latin America and Caribbean	664,997,121	0.72	4,728,047	-161,800	1.84	31	84	8.3
Northern America	378,904,407	0.54	2,033,711	1,249,364	1.64	38	82.8	4.7
Oceania	45,575,768	1.19	537,216	142,770	2.13	33	66	0.6

Source: www.worldometers.info

Table 1.3 Demographics of the 20 largest countries

Country	Population (2023)	Yearly Change (%)	Net Change	Density (P/km²)	Land Area (km²)	Net Migrants	Fertility Rate	Median Age	Urban Population (%)	World Share (%)
India	1,428,627,663	0.61	8,700,000	464	3,287,263	-532,000	2.2	28	35.2	17.9
China	1,425,887,337	-0.03	-400,000	153	9,388,211	-200,000	1.7	38	61.4	17.8
United States	334,805,269	0.38	1,268,000	36	9,147,420	900,000	1.84	38	83.6	4.2
Indonesia	277,534,122	1.07	2,930,000	151	1,904,569	-98,000	2.3	30	56.6	3.5
Pakistan	231,402,117	1.95	4,430,000	287	881,913	-233,000	3.45	23	39.5	2.9
Nigeria	223,804,632	2.53	5,520,000	237	923,768	-60,000	5.32	18	52	2.8
Brazil	214,326,223	0.51	1,090,000	25	8,515,767	21,200	1.75	33	87.6	2.7
Bangladesh	169,356,251	1.01	1,690,000	1,265	147,570	-500,000	2.15	27	38.7	2.1
Russia	142,021,000	-0.39	-552,000	9	16,376,870	182,456	1.5	40	74.9	1.8
Mexico	128,455,567	1.06	1,350,000	66	1,964,375	-60,000	2.1	29	80.7	1.6
Ethiopia	126,527,060	2.53	3,120,000	115	1,100,000	-30,000	4.15	20	22	1.6
Japan	123,508,592	-0.6	-750,000	340	364,555	71,560	1.37	48	91.8	1.5
Philippines	114,597,229	1.52	1,720,000	383	298,170	-100,000	2.75	25	47.1	1.4
Egypt	112,716,598	1.88	2,080,000	115	1,002,450	-50,000	3.28	25	43	1.4
DR Congo	102,262,000	3.19	3,160,000	46	2,344,858	-20,000	5.8	17	44	1.3

(Continues)

Table 1.3 Demographics of the 20 largest countries (Continued)

Country	Population (2023)	Yearly Change (%)	Net Change	Density (P/km²)	Land Area (km²)	Net Migrants	Fertility Rate	Median Age	Urban Population (%)	World Share (%)
Vietnam	100,388,000	0.95	950,000	311	331,212	-40,000	2.05	32	37.3	1.3
Iran	88,550,570	1.24	1,080,000	54	1,628,550	-55,000	2.15	32	76	1.1
Turkey	86,172,000	1.32	1,120,000	111	783,356	320,000	2.05	32	76.1	1.1
Germany	83,294,634	0.12	100,000	240	348,560	220,000	1.6	47	78	1.1
Thailand	70,000,000	0.25	175,000	137	513,120	19,000	1.51	39	52.9	0.9

Source: The United Nations' World Population Prospects 2024 Revision and Worldometer's live population statistics.

surge. These countries include India, Nigeria, Pakistan, the Democratic Republic of the Congo, Ethiopia, the United Republic of Tanzania, the United States, Indonesia, and Uganda. In this club, the United States is the only developed country, while the rest represent the developing or poor economies of Asia and Africa.

In sharp contrast to Africa and most parts of Asia, the populations of 48 countries and areas are expected to decline between 2025 and 2050. Many Eastern European countries, including Bulgaria, Croatia, Hungary, Latvia, Lithuania, the Republic of Moldova, Romania, Russia, Serbia, and Ukraine, as well as Japan, may experience a sharp population drop of 15 percent or more by 2050 [6, 9]. According to the *Financial Times*, Japan's population may decline as much as 31 percent by 2065 and 60 percent by 2115. This means that the population of Japan could plummet from 125 to 88 million by 2065 and to 51 million by 2115 [8xx; 10] (Table 1.3). The population decline in these countries is a result of lower fertility rates and higher median age levels over the course of the past four decades. In the past five years, 83 countries had below-replacement fertility rates while they accounted for 46 percent of the world's population.

Aging Populations

In most parts of the world, including developing countries, we have been observing two important trends: the decline in fertility rates on the one hand and the rise in life expectancy on the other hand. The outcome of these two trends is the emergence of aging populations across the world. As of 2020, the global population aged 60 years and older was approximately 1 billion, accounting for 13 percent of the total population [11]. It is projected that, by 2050, half of the global population will reside in countries where at least 20 percent of the inhabitants are aged 60 years or over [12]. The number of people aged 60 and above is expected to double between 2015 and 2050, from 960 million to 2.1 billion globally [5]. Almost 66 percent of this increase will occur in Asia, 13 percent in Africa, 11 percent in Latin America and the Caribbean, and the remaining 10percent in other regions [6]. Similarly, the number of the oldest-old or people aged 80 or over may triple by 2050 and increase more than sevenfold by the end of the century. This means that the number of people aged 80 or over is projected to increase from 125 million in 2015 to 434 million in 2050 and to 1 billion in 2100 [6].

The pace of population aging is accelerating, but it is not uniform across the globe. Europe and many developed countries, such as Japan, have been aging for decades; however, the newly industrialized countries, such as South Korea, have entered the aging phase more recently. In 2015, older adults or aged 60 and over comprised 25 percent of the population of high-income countries, 15 percent of upper-middle-income coun- tries, 9 percent of lower-middle-income countries, and 6 percent of low- income countries [13]. These figures highlight the demographic disparities between nations at different stages of economic development, with higher income countries generally having a larger proportion of older adults. Europe, with a median age of 42 years, has the oldest population, which is expected to reach 46 years by 2050. By contrast, the median age for much of the developing world is currently around 20 years and may reach 26 years by 2050. Therefore, the older populations in developed countries may grow in size, but at a much slower pace than those in newly devel- oped countries of Asia and Latin America. In the next two decades, upper middle-income countries are expected to continue to experience a rapid growth in the number of older adults. Several upper-middle-income countries are projected to become as aged as many of today's high-income countries within the next 15 years. In many developing countries, popu- lation aging is taking place much more rapidly than it did in the countries that developed earlier. For example, it took 115 years in France for the proportion of the population aged 60 years or over to increase from 7 to 14 percent [14].

In contrast, it is estimated that for Brazil, it will take just 25 years for the percentage of older people to rise from 7 to 14 percent [15]. For that reason, today's developing countries must adapt much more quickly to the aging populations and their needs. The impact of aging will be particularly noticeable in the case of Asian countries that account for large portions of the world population. For instance, by 2050, two-thirds of the world's older people will live in Asia (Figure 1.3). As mentioned previously, China and India are on very different paths of demographic change because of their dissimilar age structure and family planning policies. While China is already an aging country, India is still young and will remain so in the next few decades. Latin American and African countries are expected to have younger populations until 2050 as they still have high fertility rates and lower median age levels. Unlike all other regions, Africa is and will remain the youngest region in the forthcoming decades.

A massive aging population could involve significant implications for the labor market, personal savings, and global productivity. For instance,

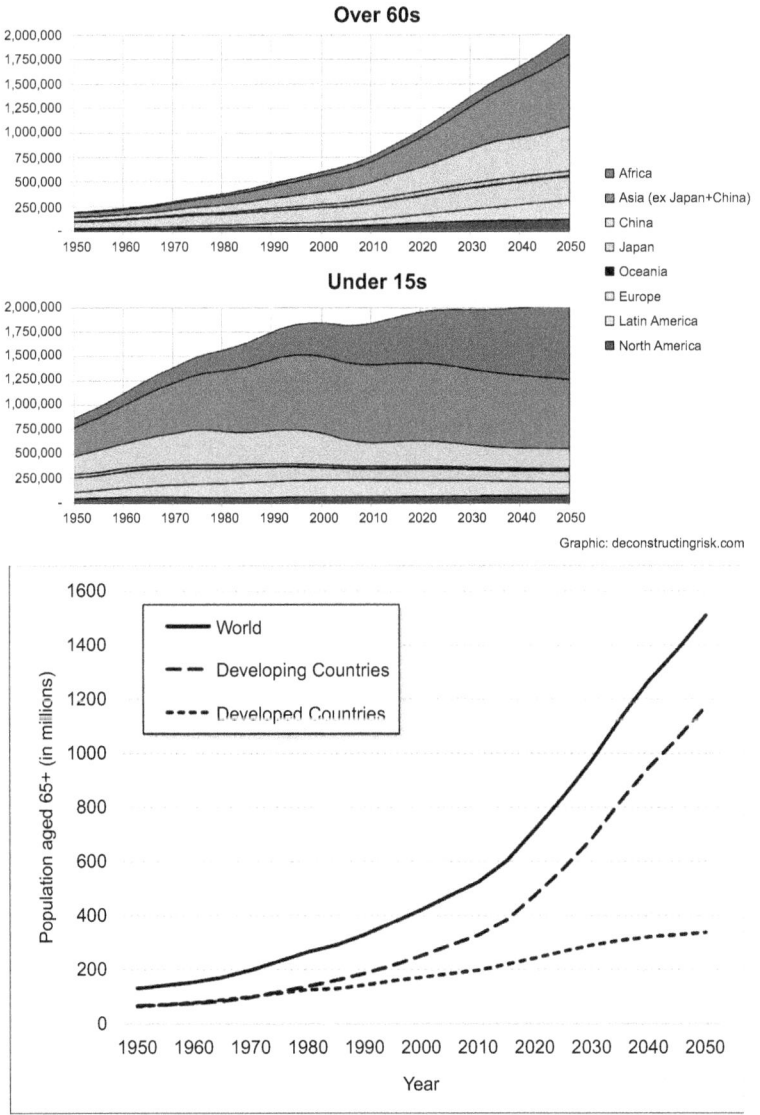

Figure 1.3 Aging populations growth by region, 1950–2050

in Europe and Japan, social protection systems, including health care and pension systems, may encounter difficulty in managing their finances. Because of aging populations, disabilities, and noncommunicable illnesses such as cardiovascular diseases, cancer, diabetes, and dementia will be rampant, causing financial pressure on public health systems. On the other hand, due to aging populations, many countries may benefit from a demographic dividend or a significant boost to their income per capita. As fertility rates decline, the burden of youth dependency reduces, the proportion of workers and savers in the population increases, and women are liberated from childbearing. In an aging society, existing resources can be allocated to building infrastructure, investing in education, and developing research and development (R&D). Indeed, the global aging in most developing countries, except in sub-Saharan Africa, is expected to result in lower levels of poverty. Nevertheless, the global aging could slow the pace of economic development in emerging economies, particularly in China, which will experience a massive shrinking of its workforce in the near future. India, unlike China, will be immune to the effects of population aging, at least for the next two decades.

Urbanization: 2.5 Billion Will Be Urbanized by 2050

Owing to the widespread socioeconomic development over the past six decades, the world has experienced rapid urbanization. The world's population is constantly becoming more urbanized as cities are attracting a large number of inhabitants. For the first time in 2007, the world's urban population surpassed the world's rural population. According to the World Bank reports, the share of the world's urban population has risen from 30 percent in 1950 to more than 57 percent in 2023 [16]. The trend toward urbanization is expected to persist, with projections indicating that 68 percent of the world's population will reside in urban areas by 2050. The ongoing urbanization in conjunction with the growth of the global population will add 2.5 billion people to the urban population by 2050, with nearly 90 percent of the increase concentrated in Asia and Africa [17].

As of 2023, North America and Latin America remain the most urbanized regions globally, with urbanization rates exceeding 80 percent. Specifically, North America's urbanization rate is approximately 83.15 percent, while Latin America and the Caribbean have an urbanization rate of about 81.8 percent [18]. In the same year, Europe's rate of urban settlement was close to 75 percent, while Africa and Asia were mostly rural with urban settlement rates of 53 and 45 percent, respectively [26]. As of 2023, many countries still had low levels of urbanization of 20 percent or less, including Burundi, Malawi, Niger, South Sudan, and Uganda in Africa, and Nepal and Sri Lanka in Asia [18].

There are considerable disparities between developed and developing countries about the urbanization process. For instance, most developed countries underwent urbanization in the 1960s and 1970s, with the urban share of their total populations rising from 47 percent in the 1960s to 60 percent in the early 1980s, before plateauing. At present, more than 75 percent of the populations in developing countries still live in rural areas, suggesting that the sharpest increase in the urban centers will happen in such countries. Based on the United Nations estimates, almost 2.5 billion people will be added to the global urban population by 2050. Of these 2.5 billion new urban dwellers, almost 90 percent will live in Africa and Asia. Only three countries, namely India, China, and Nigeria, are expected to account for more than one-third of global urban population growth [19]. Seven other countries, notably the Democratic Republic of the Congo, Ethiopia, the United Republic of Tanzania, Bangladesh, Indonesia, Pakistan, and the United States, will account for another 20 percent of the growth of the global urban population [19]. In some Asian countries, such as China and Korea, urbanization accompanied economic development. However, in many other countries, including Pakistan, Haiti, and the Democratic Republic of the Congo, urbanization happened in the absence of socioeconomic development and despite dysfunctional politics [20]. Indeed, a remarkable trend in the contemporary world is the rapid urbanization in developing and poor nations. For example, in the 1960s, most of the poor nations were rural with urbanization rates of less than 25 percent. In recent years, the majority of poor countries have urbanized. According to the United Nations, the urbanization rate in developing countries increased from 18 percent in 1950 to 47 percent in 2011 and 55 percent in 2023 [17].

The urbanization phenomenon has resulted in the emergence of the vast urban centers or "megacities" with more than 10 million people. By 2030, the world is projected to have 41 cities with more than 10 million inhabitants [21]. In this category, Tokyo (38 million), Jakarta (34 million), Delhi (32 million), Shanghai (29 million), Sao Paulo (23 million), Cairo (23 million), Mumbai (22 million), and Mexico City (22 million) are ranked as the most significant cities. These figures underscore the rapid expansion of urban centers, particularly in Asia and Africa, where cities are experiencing unprecedented growth rates. This urbanization presents both opportunities and challenges, including the need for sustainable infrastructure, housing, and services to accommodate the increasing urban populations.

Several decades ago, most of the world's largest cities were located in the developed countries. However, currently large urban centers are found or are being formed in the developing countries of Asia (Table 1.4). The megacities involve significant social and economic consequences as some of them like Tokyo (38 million) and Delhi (32 million) are comparable to sizable countries such as Canada (40 million) and Australia (26 million). The proliferation of such large cities may put a strain on environmental resources, including air, water, soil, and ecological systems.

Urbanization, particularly in the lower-middle-income countries where the pace of urbanization is fastest, may cause substantial socio-economic challenges. Nevertheless, urban centers can offer advantageous services to a large number of people. For instance, health care, education, public transportation, housing, electricity, water, and sanitation are generally available to urban dwellers in a pretty effective manner [22]. Populations move to large cities because they are the centers of trade, foreign direct investments (FDIs), and economic development. Urban dwellers have better access to larger and more diversified labor markets, which in turn enables them to enjoy healthier lives. The life expectancy in urban centers is generally higher, while the fertility rate is significantly lower. An important pattern is that as countries urbanize, their overall total fertility rates decline because the fertility rates in urban centers are much lower than those in rural areas [23].

Table 1.4 The world's largest metropolitan areas (as of 2023)

Rank	Metropolitan Area	Population
1	Tokyo-Yokohama, Japan	37,785,000
2	Jakarta, Indonesia	35,386,000
3	Delhi, India	31,190,000
4	Guangzhou-Foshan, China	27,119,000
5	Mumbai, India	25,189,000
6	Manila, Philippines	24,156,000
7	Shanghai, China	24,042,000
8	Seoul-Incheon, South Korea	23,225,000
9	Cairo, Egypt	22,679,000
10	Mexico City, Mexico	21,905,000
11	Kolkata, India	21,747,000
12	São Paulo, Brazil	21,486,000
13	New York, USA	19,563,798
14	Beijing, China	19,000,000
15	Lagos, Nigeria	18,000,000
16	Bangkok, Thailand	17,000,000
17	Dhaka, Bangladesh	16,000,000
18	Karachi, Pakistan	15,000,000
19	Buenos Aires, Argentina	15,000,000
20	Istanbul, Turkey	15,000,000
21	Los Angeles, USA	12,870,137
22	Rio de Janeiro, Brazil	12,000,000
23	Shenzhen, China	12,000,000
24	Kinshasa, DR Congo	11,000,000
25	Tianjin, China	11,000,000
26	Paris, France	11,000,000
27	Lima, Peru	10,000,000
28	Chengdu, China	10,000,000
29	Lahore, Pakistan	10,000,000
30	Bangalore, India	10,000,000

Source: [24]

Global Migration

Demographic trends and international migratory movements are closely correlated. Europe, Northern America, and Australia are net receivers of international migrants because they have lower fertility rates and higher median age levels. On the contrary, Africa, Asia, Latin America, and the Caribbean countries are net senders of international migrants because they have much higher fertility rates and lower median age levels.

Over the past decade, Europe and North America have experienced significant immigration flows. For instance, Europe received an estimated total of 28 million immigrants from non-EU (European Union) countries over the past 10 years [25]. Similarly, over the past 10 years, the United States has admitted approximately 10 million immigrants, while Canada has welcomed another 3.5 million immigrants [26]. Europe and North America contain 15 percent of the global population but are home to more than half of the world's international migrants. In addition to the diverging demographic trends between developed and developing countries, geopolitical turmoil, war, conflict, and invasion in the Middle East and Asia will contribute to the increasing influx of populations from poor to rich countries in the next four decades. The demographic forces are the main drivers of international migration. However, the economic factors also have important implications because the direction of migration is always from the less developed and low-income countries to the developed and high-income ones. In the next four decades, the United States, Canada, the United Kingdom, Australia, Germany, the Russian Federation, and Italy are expected to be the top receivers of international migrants [27]. During the same period, sub-Saharan Africa, India, Bangladesh, China, Pakistan, and Mexico are expected to be the top sources of international migrants. In the current globalized world, skilled and educated migrants are privileged over unskilled and uneducated ones. The international migration flows are affected by multiple constraints set in developed countries' laws. Therefore, in comparison with the historical large-scale migrations, the recent international migratory movements are more selective.

It is widely accepted that migration has adverse effects on labor supply in developing countries, as most of the emigrants come from the educated and skilled workforce [27]. Instead, the sending countries may benefit from the remittances that migrants send back to their countries of origin. Because of increasing economic development in emerging countries, the migration flows from South to North may change to a South-to-South migration pattern. Some emerging countries with high economic growth rates could attract a large number of migrant workers from low-income neighboring countries. Climate change, desertification, destruction of farmland, resource scarcity, air and water pollution, terrorism, and regional conflicts may create new patterns of international migration among the Southern and low-income countries. For example, due to the Syrian conflict, about 3.2 million Syrians have fled their homeland and have migrated to Turkey. The flight of more than 1 million Syrians to Europe in 2015, perhaps one of the largest mass migrations in recent history, shows that the patterns of international migration are becoming more complex and unpredictable.

Migration is becoming a key contributor to population growth in high-income countries, as migrants from low-income countries often have higher birth rates than the host population. For example, the average fertility rates of migrants in Europe and the United States are significantly higher than the national averages. Furthermore, by reducing median age levels, migration can indirectly influence the population size and age structure of receiving countries. Migration increases the total dependency ratio of sender countries and reduces their share of the working-age population. On the other hand, in receiving countries, migration increases the share of the working population and reduces old-age dependency [28].

The Demographics of Faith and Religious Denominations: The Revival of God

The differences in fertility rates and median age levels among the world's major religions are working to change the global religious composition. While many sociologists had predicted the end of religion in the 19th and 20th centuries, the world as a whole has become more religious in the past four decades. For instance, the share of religious people has grown from 82 percent in 1970 to 88 percent in 2024 [29]. Religiousness is growing mainly due to demographic trends because religious communities have higher fertility rates and procreate more than the average person. As of 2023, the global number of religiously unaffiliated individuals, including atheists and agnostics, is estimated to be approximately 1.2 billion. This number represents a modest increase from the 1.1 billion reported in 2010 [30]. Atheists and other people who do not affiliate with any religion are expected to increase in absolute number, particularly in Western countries such as France, Germany, and the United States. However, they will constitute a declining share of the world's population because of the twofold demographic disadvantages of low fertility rates and old-age structures. As a consequence, the share of religiously unaffiliated people is expected to decline from 16 percent in 2010 to 13 percent by 2050 [30].

As of 2023, Christianity and Islam remain the world's two largest religions. Christianity has approximately 2.4 billion adherents, accounting for about 31 percent of the global population, while Islam has around 1.9 billion followers, representing roughly 25 percent. Combined, these two faiths encompass over half of the world's population (Table 1.5). Christianity is and will remain the largest religious group in the next four decades. However, Islam is growing faster than any other major religion and is expected to overtake Christianity as the largest religious denomination after 2050 [31]. According to the Pew Research projections, the adherents of Christianity are expected to grow, but their growth will be slower, and they will constitute 35 percent of the global population by 2050 [31]. As of 2023, the global Jewish population was approximately 15.7 million, reflecting a gradual increase from the estimated 14 million in 2010. In the United States, the share of Christians will decline from 75 percent of the population in 2010 to 66 percent in 2050, and Muslims will be more numerous in the United States than the adherents of Judaism will. Unlike all other major religions, the number of Buddhist adherents is expected to be constant because of low fertility rates and aging populations in countries such as China and Japan. At the same time, the Hindu population is estimated to surge from 1 to 1.4 billion by 2050, representing an increase of roughly 40 percent. There are important geographic disparities in the patterns of religious growth in the coming decades. For example, the religiously unaffiliated population will be concentrated in Europe and North America and will increase as a share of the population in these areas.

On the other hand, most of the global growth in the number of Muslims and Christians is expected to happen in the low-income and sub-Saharan African countries, characterized by low median ages and high fertility rates. Consistent with these estimates, more than 40 percent of the world's Christians will reside in sub-Saharan Africa by 2050. The rapid changes in religious identities may involve important implications

Table 1.5 Major world religions

Religious Affiliation	Share of World Population (%)	Population Estimate
Christian	31.10	2.4 billion
Catholic	15.90	1.2 billion
Protestant	6.00	900 million
Orthodox	3.70	280 million
Muslim	24.90	1.9 billion
Sunni	20.40	1.6 billion
Shia	4.50	285 million
Unaffiliated (Includes Atheists and Agnostics)	15.60	1.2 billion
Hindu	15.20	1.2 billion
Buddhist	6.60	506 million
Folk Religionist	5.60	430 million
Other Religions (Baha'i, Taoism, Jainism, Shintoism, Sikhism, Zoroastrianism, and others.)	0.80	61 million
Jewish	0.20	14 million

Source: The Pew Research Center [31]

for different spheres of life, including politics, the legal system, family, education, and technology [29]. Furthermore, the growing disparities among the major religious denominations may lead to cultural collisions, social or geopolitical tensions, conflicts, and political turmoil.

The Languages of Present and Future

Currently, there are almost 7,000 languages spoken across the world, but a large number of these languages have limited scopes and some are facing the risk of disappearance [32]. The linguistic diversity is under increasing pressure, as 50 to 90 percent of the world's languages are predicted to become extinct by the end of the 21st century [32]. Because of globalization and advances in telecommunication and transport, the world as a whole is becoming linguistically and culturally less diverse than ever. Currently, 15 languages dominate the global stage because they constitute the mother tongues of half of the world's population. At the top is Mandarin Chinese with almost 1 billion native speakers, followed by Spanish, which is the second most common mother tongue of 500 million people. English ranks third, with over 450 million native speakers, followed by Hindi and Arabic, which share the fourth and fifth places with almost 300 million native speakers. While the number of native speakers is an important criterion in determining the power of a language, other variables such as geography, economy, communication, knowledge, media, and diplomacy seem relevant in evaluating the present and future influence of a language. Relying on these criteria, the 10 most dominant languages may be ranked as English, Mandarin, French, Spanish, Arabic, Russian, German, Japanese, Portuguese, and Hindi (Table 1.6). With an estimated 450 million native speakers, English is considered the most important language. Indeed, English is the dominant language of the world's largest economy (the United States) and other large economies such as the United Kingdom, Canada, and Australia. English will remain the global lingua franca at least for the next three decades, and its native speakers will reach 540 million by 2050. Mandarin is becoming an important language, not only because of the large number of its native speakers but also because of the growing Chinese economy that has become the world's second largest after the United States. While the number of French native speakers is close to 80 million, French is considered the third most influential language in the world due to its geopolitical impact on Africa and its importance in diplomacy and international affairs.

It is almost impossible to predict the future of languages, but the power of a language depends highly on the number of its native and foreign speakers. Accordingly, English will remain the most influential language in the world with close to 550 million native speakers at least by 2050. By 2050, there will not be any sizable growth in the number of native speakers of Mandarin, French, Russian, German, and Japanese. Indeed, these languages are spoken in countries with very low birth rates due to their socioeconomic conditions, and as a result, they will not experience significant demographic increases. By contrast, the native speakers of languages such as Spanish, Arabic, Hindi, and Portuguese are expected to experience significant growth by 2050. According to a report by the British Council, Hindi, Bengali, Urdu, Indonesian, Spanish, Portuguese, Arabic, and Russian will be some important languages for doing business in the next three decades [33].

Table 1.6 The most powerful languages

Rank	Score	Language	Native (MM)	Geography	Economy	Communication	Knowledge and Media	Diplomacy
1	0.889	English	446.0	1	1	1	1	1
2	0.411	Mandarin	960.0	6	2	2	3	6
3	0.337	French	80.00	2	6	5	5	1
4	0.329	Spanish	470.0	3	5	3	7	3
5	0.273	Arabic	295.0	4	9	6	18	4
6	0.244	Russian	150.0	5	12	10	9	5
7	0.191	German	92.5	8	3	7	4	8
8	0.133	Japanese	125.0	27	4	22	6	7
9	0.119	Portuguese	215.0	7	19	13	12	9
10	0.117	Hindi	310.0	13	16	8	2	10

References

[1] Population Division. 2024. "World Urbanization Prospects: The 2024 Revision." United Nations, Department of Economic and Social Affairs.

[2] https://www.worldometers.info/world-population

[3] https://www.worldometers.info/world-population/asia-population/

[4] United Nations. Dept of Economics. 2003. *World Population Prospects: The 2002 Revision. Sex and age.* No. 222-223. United Nations Publications.

[5] Japan's Population Set to Fall to 88m by 2065. https://ft.com/content/00df659e-1dcf-11e7-a454-ab04428977f9 (accessed June 18, 2017).

[6] Parkes, R. 2015. "The European Union and the Geopolitics of Migration." UI Paper no. 1/2015.

[7] https://www.who.int/data/gho/data/indicators/indicator-details/GHO/population-proportion-over-60-%28-%29

[8] Nations, U. 2013. World Population Aging 2013. Department of Economic and Social Affairs PD.

[9] Bloom, D.E. 2016. "Demographic Upheaval." *Finance and Development* 53, no. 1, pp. 6–11.

[10] Dahlman, O. 2025. "Global Population." In *Securing Our Future: A Science-Based Approach to Global Threats*, 35-47. Cham: Springer Nature Switzerland.

[11] World Health Organization. https://www.who.int/news-room/fact-sheets/detail/ageing-and-health

[12] Kinsella, K.G., and Y.J. Gist. 1995. Older Workers, Retirement, and Pensions: A Comparative International Chartbook (No. 95). US Department of Commerce, Economics and Statistics Administration, Bureau of the Census.

[13] Naja, S., M.M.E.D. Makhlouf, and M.A.H Chehab. 2017. "An Ageing World of the 21st Century: A Literature Review." *The International Journal of Community Medicine and Public Health*, 4, no. 12, pp. 4363–4369.

[14] Nations, U. 2023. Leaving No One Behind in an Ageing World. *World Social Report.*

[15] de Azeredo Passos, V.M., A.P.S. Champs, R. Teixeira, M.F.F. Lima-Costa, R. Kirkwood, R. Veras, ... & F.M. Souza. 2020. The Burden of Disease Among Brazilian Older Adults and the Challenge for Health Policies: Results of the Global Burden of Disease Study 2017. *Population health metrics*, 18, Suppl 1, p. 14.

[16] World Bank. https://data.worldbank.org/indicator/SP.URB.TOTL.IN.ZS

[17] United Nations. https://www.un.org/en/desa/around-25-billion-more-people-will-be-living-cities-2050-projects-new-un-report

[18] Anestis, G., and D. Stathakis. 2024. "Urbanization Trends from the Global to the Local Scale." In *Geographical Information Science*, 357–375. Elsevier.

[19] Prasad, S. 2019. "Why the World Should be Watching India's Fast-Growing Cities." In *the World Economic Forum.*

[20] Myers, G. 2021. "Urbanisation in the Global South." In *Urban ecology in the Global South*, 27–49. Cham: Springer International Publishing.

[21] Hoornweg, D., and K. Pope. 2017. Population Predictions for the World's Largest Cities in the 21st Century. *Environment and urbanization* 29, no.1, pp. 195–216.

[22] World Health Organization. https://www.who.int/health-topics/urban-health#tab=tab_1

[23] Nargund, G. 2009. Declining Birth Rate in Developed Countries: A Radical Policy Rethink is Required. *Facts, Views & Vision in ObGyn* 1, no. 3, p. 191.

[24] https://www.statista.com/statistics/912263/population-of-urban-agglomerations-worldwide/

[25] Boswell, C. 2018. "Migration in Europe." In *Politics of Migration*, 91–110. Routledge.

[26] Statistics Canada. 2022. Immigrants Make Up the Largest Share of the Population in Over 150 Years and Continue to Shape Who We Are as Canadians." *The Daily* 1, no. 11, pp. 1–21.

[27] Czaika, M., and C. Reinprecht. 2020. "Drivers of Migration: A Synthesis of Knowledge." *IMI Working Paper Series* 163, pp. 1–45.

[28   Mackie, C., and F.D. Blau (eds.). 2017. *The Economic and Fiscal Consequences of Immigration*. National Academies Press.

[29] Norris, P., and R. Inglehart. 2011. *Sacred and Secular: Religion and Politics Worldwide*. Cambridge University Press.

[30] Hackett, C., M. Stonawski, Y. Tong, S. Kramer, A. Shi, and D. Fahmy. 2025. How the Global Religious Landscape Changed From 2010 to 2020.

[31] https://www.pewforum.org/wp-content/uploads/sites/7/2021/12/PF_12.14.21_update_on_religion_trends_report.pdf?utm_source=chatgpt.com15

[32] Noack, R. 2015. The Future of Language. *The Washington Post*. https://washingtonpost.com/news/worldviews/wp/2015/09/24/the-future-of-language/?utm_term=.eec17bd2e40f (accessed August 20, 2017).

[33] The Washington Post, The Future of Language https://www.washingtonpost.com/news/worldviews/wp/2015/09/24/the-future-of-language/

CHAPTER 2

Globalization: Transformations and Consequences

Different Views on Globalization

Globalization can be defined as a process that fosters greater interdependence and mutual awareness among the economic, political, and social units of the world [1–4]. It is a complex phenomenon characterized by the increasing cross-border movement of goods, services, capital, people, and information [1, 4]. Because of this complexity, globalization is far from universally embraced; it is accompanied by persistent conflicts among social groups, nation-states, and hegemonic powers [5]. It constitutes aweb of interconnections that transcend national borders and local communities, creating conditions in which events, decisions, and activities in one part of the world can produce significant consequences elsewhere [6]. In doing so, globalization disrupts traditional linkages between territoriality and authority, shifting decision-making power from national and local levels to more universal, transnational arenas [7]. This shift enables the emergence of a networked society, facilitating real-time interactions across the globe despite temporal and spatial limitations.

Although globalization has historical roots reaching back to ancient times, its modern usage is primarily associated with the rapid sociotechnological transformations of the late 20th century [1] (Table 2.1). Historically, its expansion coincided with the end of the Cold War, though it remains unclear whether the relationship between these events is causal [8]. It is possible that détente between the United States and the Soviet Union created a more favorable environment for global trade and the exchange of ideas.

Table 2.1 The multiple views on globalization, their meanings, features, and consequences

Perspective	Central Idea	Features and Consequences
Economic	A global marketplace for production, distribution, and consumption	Liberalization and deregulation of markets Privatization of assets Financial deregulation Cross-national production Integration of capital markets
Cultural	An increasing convergence in the world's cultural values	Homogenization of all cultural values Prevalence of modernization Acceptance of capitalism and liberal democracy
Sociotechno-logical	A connection of the local communities together so they can function in a coherent planetary system	Unprecedented explosion of information, products, and services Reconciliation between the local and global
Business	Glocalization of business activities	Reproduction of international businesses on a regional or local basis
Sociological	A compression of temporal and spatial dimensions	Dialectical linkage of distant localities: Reflexivity

Economically, globalization signifies a structural shift away from national economies toward an integrated global marketplace for production, distribution, and consumption [9, 10]. This transformation has been marked by developments such as market liberalization and deregulation, privatization of assets, the creation of cross-national production networks, and the integration of global capital markets [11].

Culturally, globalization is often seen as a process of convergence, fostering the homogenization of societies regardless of their historical and cultural distinctiveness (Table 2.1). Over the past half-century, most countries have experienced deep socioeconomic transformations, including increased state centralization, urbanization, universal education, and higher literacy rates. From this perspective, globalization facilitates a form of modernization grounded in capitalist principles and liberal democratic values, often reflecting the American interpretation of Enlightenment ideals [12]. It can also be viewed as a social revolution propelled by technological innovation, reshaping the world into a single, integrated market [12]. As Castells argues, globalization connects local communities in ways that enable them to operate cohesively within a planetary system [2]. In recent decades, this process has been accompanied by a paradigmatic shift in our understanding of social and economic relations, along with the restructuring of economic activity at regional and local levels, and a massive surge in the flow of information, goods, and services across borders [12].

This global–local interplay has given rise to the concept of *glocalization*—a fusion of global and local elements. Multinational corporations often adopt glocalization strategies, tailoring products and operations to local markets while maintaining centralized control. Such an approach enables firms to be perceived as local entities without relinquishing authority to regional subsidiaries.

From a sociological standpoint, globalization can also be understood as a compression of time and space [13, 14], heightening global awareness and enabling reciprocal communication and interaction. Giddens (1990) characterizes it as a dialectical and interactive process in which distant localities become interconnected, allowing local events to be shaped by distant occurrences and vice versa [14]. In this sense, globalization is often regarded as an unfinished, fluid, and intermittent process, generating a range of contradictory effects and implications [2, 15, 16].

Globalization of Culture: Convergence, Divergence, and Cultural Mélange

Cultural Convergence

In today's interconnected world, the flow of consumer goods, labor, capital, technology, people, and—most critically—ideas occurs across borders with unprecedented ease and speed. Multinational corporations increasingly leverage their economic power to bypass institutional and legal constraints imposed by nation-states. As a result, global consumers now commonly watch the same television programs, listen to the same pop music, purchase global brand products, and wear similar styles of clothing [1, 2]. Advances in computerized networks have accelerated the cross-border movement of information, dissolving traditional barriers of geography, language, and ethnicity [3].

These dynamics push societies around the world toward embracing the value systems characteristic of established Western capitalist economies. Local cultures, increasingly exposed to dominant global influences, often face erosion of their distinct identities and become assimilated into a broader, global culture [1, 4]. This process of homogenization is what proponents of the convergence perspective refer to as cultural convergence. According to Ritzer (2008), this often amounts to the "Americanization" of local cultures, wherein U.S. cultural values—shaped by the country's economic and technological preeminence—dominate global cultural landscapes [1, 4].

The United States, for example, plays a central role in global telecommunications and digital infrastructure: 85 percent of all web pages originate in the United States, and American firms control roughly 75 percent of the global packaged software market [1, 5]. Moreover, U.S. culture continues to dominate the global entertainment, media, and music industries. This one-directional cultural flow from the West, particularly from the United States, to the rest of the world is perceived by many as a form of cultural imperialism. Critics in developing countries often view this homogenization as a disruptive force—an encroachment of global capitalism that undermines their indigenous cultures, religions, traditions, and collective identities [1, 6–8].

Cultural Divergence

In contrast, the divergence perspective emphasizes cultural heterogeneity. It argues that globalization has not led to cultural uniformity but has instead heightened the awareness of cultural differences. As people become increasingly conscious of their unique cultural identities, they often take pride in preserving them. Globalization, paradoxically, can reinforce the question of identity—"Who am I?"—and spark efforts to maintain local traditions and values [9, 10].

Rather than submitting to cultural convergence, many communities actively resist the influence of dominant global cultures. Intellectuals in developing nations often argue that globalization is not a balanced exchange but a form of cultural domination, wherein the values, norms, and products of Western societies are imposed upon others [11,12]. They express concern about transformations in consumption habits, language use, clothing styles, ideals of beauty, educational models, and sexual norms. Rapid shifts in cultural identity can cause psychological disorientation and social fragmentation. In response, some local communities strengthen their adherence to traditional practices and norms as a form of resistance. Thus, globalization does not inevitably lead to cultural sameness; it also stimulates divergence, as communities strive to protect and affirm their distinctiveness.

Cultural Hybridization (Mélange)

The third perspective—cultural hybridization or mélange—recognizes the complex interplay between convergence and divergence. This view critiques the simplistic binaries of homogenization and heterogenization by focusing on how global cultural elements are locally received, adapted, and transformed [12–14]. Rather than being passively absorbed, global cultural forms are selectively integrated into local contexts, resulting in hybrid cultural identities that are neither fully global nor purely local [4].

Cultural hybridization reflects a dynamic process in which global and local cultures interact to produce new cultural configurations. These hybrid forms may blend global trends with traditional practices, creating unique cultural expressions that defy straightforward categorization [12, 15]. As such, globalization generates a mosaic of sociocultural forms rather than a single global culture.

This blending process also challenges rigid notions of ethnicity, localness, and tradition, leading to the emergence of fluid and overlapping cultural landscapes [1, 16]. While surface-level cultural artifacts—such as food, fashion, or entertainment—may be easily hybridized, deeper layers of culture, such as fundamental beliefs and value systems, often remain more resistant to change. Consequently, globalization simultaneously drives processes of both convergence and divergence, depending on the cultural layers involved [1, 17].

Cultural hybridization may be a source of enrichment. Throughout history, some of the world's most vibrant cultural traditions emerged at the intersections of distinct civilizations—for instance, in Athens, the Indus Valley, and Mesoamerica. These historical examples illustrate how cross-cultural interaction can foster innovation, diversity, and creativity [18].

Globalization and the Changing Role of Nation-States

Globalization denationalizes the markets, opens the door to international competition, and eventually pushes nation-states to react to international forces rather than to the domestic population. Therefore, nation-states become increasingly responsive to the global community [17]. Economic integration empowers international organizations to make direct decisions on fiscal and monetary policies, trade, tariffs, environmental issues, and interest rates. Globalization restrains nation-states from taxing, spend, and controlling their domestic affairs. Moreover, globalization, by facilitating the cross-border movements of labor and capital, loosens government control and makes national borders less relevant. In addition to the strong supranational institutions, large corporations and powerful businesses exert significant pressure on the ability of nation-states to function properly [2]. Nations and their citizens become hostages of supranational markets, international lenders, and investment banks. Globalization weakens the ability of nation-states to regulate what happens on their own land. Thus, it is plausible to suggest that, by creating a constant tension between national and supranational forces, globalization and the ensuing economic integration undermine the traditional roles of nation-states. The advocates of globalization believe that economic integration affects the nation-states, but does not destroy them. As a solution, the nation-states should become more resilient and agile to benefit from the economic effects of globalization. Some go further and argue that nation-states should not fear globalization, as the global forces ultimately serve the interests of citizens. This argument advocates that globalization is a continuation of capitalist development; therefore, those nation-states that become more globalized are more likely to become prosperous.

Regardless of the perspective that we adopt, it is evident that globalization undermines the traditional functions of the nation-state, particularly in the case of smaller countries that do not have abundant financial resources and large populations. Furthermore, the large multinational corporations and many other global institutions, such as the International Monetary Fund (IMF), the World Trade Organization (WTO), and the

World Bank, are not restrained by any democratic legitimacy or social accountability. The financial crises in Greece and Ireland showed that the smaller nation-states are incapable of exerting their sovereign rights during financial hardship or extended periods of distress; instead, they become entirely dependent on supranational institutions to avoid the risk of collapse.

The aforementioned discussion leads us to three important conclusions. First, the effects of globalization on nation-states are inevitable because these effects are the direct consequences of temporal and spatial compression. Second, globalization and economic integration could serve the interests of nation-states. The more globalized nation-states are generally more successful, influential, and prosperous. Therefore, globalization might change the role of nation-states, but it does not necessarily undermine their power. Third, in the game of globalization, some nation-states could be winners as they gain power and influence, while others could be losers as they continue to decline. In addition to these three conclusions, the changing role of nation-states offers an opportunity for the creation of a system of global governance where important issues such as environmental degradation, climate change, overpopulation, and international security can be effectively tackled.

A New Balance of Economic Power

Over the past four decades, the globalization of trade and production has been a major driver of wealth creation worldwide. Despite significant disruptions—most notably the global financial crisis of 2007–2008 and the COVID-19 pandemic—international trade has continued to expand. Between 2010 and 2022, global trade in goods grew by more than 50 percent, fueled in large part by the increasing participation of developing countries in global commerce [19]. A striking feature of this transformation is the rapid rise of South–South trade, which now accounts for over 30 percent of global trade. In terms of merchandise exchange, South–South flows have nearly equaled North–North trade [20].

One of the key structural changes underpinning this growth is the fragmentation of production and the rise of global value chains (GVCs). Cross-border trade in intermediate or unfinished goods has become central to the global economy, accounting for approximately 52–55 percent of world trade as of 2022 [21]. This shift reflects a more profound economic interdependence and a reconfiguration of supply networks, with production processes increasingly spread across multiple countries.

Historically, early 20th-century trade was dominated by a handful of Western powers—most notably the United States, the United Kingdom, France, Germany, and the Netherlands [22]. In recent decades, however, this concentration of economic power has been eroded by the rapid rise of the Global South, particularly China, India, South Korea, Brazil, and South Africa.

The most dramatic example of this shift is China. Its share of global GDP has surged from just 2 percent in 1980 to over 18 percent in 2023 [23]. Over the same period, the U.S. share of global output fell from 27.3 percent in the 1950s to around 15.5 percent in 2023. Japan's share declined to under 5 percent, while the EU's contribution dropped from about 30 percent in the 1980s to just over 14 percent in 2023 [24]. Significant improvements in living standards have accompanied this transformation: China's GDP per capita rose from $318 in 1990 to more than $12,500 in 2022 [24]. India's GDP per capita increased from $370 in 1990 to over $2,400 in 2022, and even sub-Saharan Africa experienced gains, from $627 in 2004 to over $1,650 in 2022 [23].

Current projections suggest that by 2030, Organization for Economic Cooperation and Development (OECD) countries will account for less than half of global output, with emerging economies—led by China, India, ASEAN members, and Latin American states—commanding an ever-larger share [25]. This rebalancing of economic power is one of globalization's most profound consequences.

As their economic weight grows, emerging economies are becoming more assertive in shaping global governance. The rising influence of Eastern and Southern nations challenges the long-standing dominance of Western Europe and North America, forcing advanced economies to undertake complex structural adjustments. These measures—often involving austerity programs, deindustrialization, and labor market reforms—have fueled public discontent across many Western societies.

This dissatisfaction has, in turn, contributed to the rise of right-wing and populist political movements, which have capitalized on

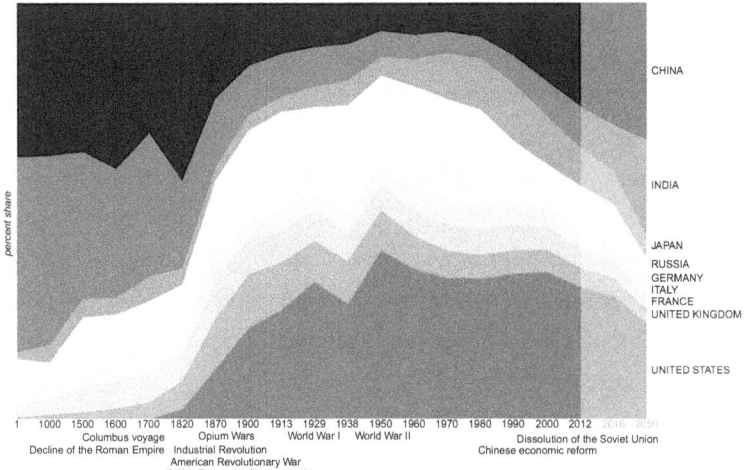

Figure 2.1 **A new balance of economic power: Past, present, and future (based on the share of the combined GDP of the nine countries)**

Source: GDP data for years 1-2000: Angus Maddison, University of Groningen; 2016 IMF-projected GDP growth; 2050 PricewaterhouseCoopers-projected GDP growth.

antiglobalization sentiments and pushed for more protectionist and interventionist policies. These political realignments reflect deep-seated anxieties over the erosion of traditional economic privileges and geopolitical influence in the West.

While globalization continues to foster interdependence and overall economic growth, it is also driving a fundamental shift toward a more multipolar global economy. This transition not only offers opportunities for more balanced development but also introduces new strategic and political challenges as the distribution of power becomes more diffuse.

Globalization and Pressure on Social Welfare

The globalization of production has allowed multinational corporations to disperse their value chain activities worldwide, capitalizing on location-specific advantages such as low labor costs, abundant natural resources, and advanced technological infrastructure. Since the 1990s, breakthroughs in telecommunications and digital technologies have accelerated this trend, prompting a large-scale relocation of manufacturing from industrialized economies to lower-cost regions, particularly in

Asia. This wave of offshoring has led to substantial job losses and under-employment in the manufacturing sectors of developed countries, while exerting downward pressure on wages.

In the United States, industries directly competing with low-cost imports have been especially hard-hit, with workers experiencing significant job displacement and wage stagnation [26]. Simultaneously, trade liberalization has reduced tariff revenues and corporate tax income, constraining government budgets. These fiscal pressures have often translated into cutbacks in social protection programs, disproportionately affecting low- and semiskilled workers [27].

Many Western governments have responded by scaling back welfare provisions, including pensions, unemployment insurance, and child care services. However, most European nations—particularly France, Spain, and Italy—have resisted wage suppression and maintained robust social safety nets, prioritizing income equality. While socially protective, this approach has reduced labor cost competitiveness and contributed to persistently high unemployment rates in recent years.

The U.S. experience contrasts sharply: relatively lower unemployment rates have been accompanied by widening wage inequality and stagnant earnings, especially for workers with lower levels of education [28]. The adverse wage effects of globalization have been most severe for low-skilled manufacturing workers, whose jobs are highly susceptible to outsourcing and automation. These workers are widely regarded as the primary casualties of globalization. In contrast, high-skilled professionals—whose roles are less vulnerable to offshoring—often benefit through increased demand for their expertise and expanded mobility opportunities.

In developing countries, the effects of globalization have been more mixed. A subset of emerging economies with stable institutions and favorable investment climates—such as parts of East Asia—have achieved significant gains from global trade and FDI. However, many other developing nations, lacking strong legal, political, and economic frameworks, have failed to capitalize on globalization's opportunities. In some cases, these countries have experienced not only deindustrialization but also a decline in traditional agricultural sectors, resulting in economic contraction rather than growth.

As Nobel Laureate Joseph Stiglitz cautions, globalization and market liberalization can undermine productivity and employment in nations without the institutional capacity to manage economic transitions effectively [28]. In such contexts, rather than fostering development, globalization risks deepening inequality, eroding productive capacity, and obstructing pathways to sustainable growth.

References

[1] Held, D., A. McGrew, D. Goldblatt, and J. Perraton. 1999. *Global Transformations*. Stanford, CA: Stanford University Press.

[2] Guillen, M.F. 2001. "Is Globalization Civilizing, Destructive or Feeble? A Critique of Five Key Debates in the Social Science Literature." *Annual Review of Sociology* 27, no. 1, pp. 235–60.

[3] Petrella, R. 1996. "Globalization and Internationalization." In *States Against Markets: The Limits of Globalization*, 62–83. London: Routledge.

[4] Steger, M.B. 2010. *Globalization*, 63. John Wiley & Sons, Ltd. NJ, USA,

[5] Santos, B.D.S. 2002. "The Processes of Globalisation." In *Revista Critica de Ciencias Sociais and Eurozine*, 1–48. Coimbra, Portugal

[6] McGrew, A. 1990. "A Global Society." In *Modernity and Its Futures*, eds. S. Hall, D. Held, and A. McGrew. *Modernity and its futures* (pp. xx–xx). Cambridge, UK: Polity Press / Open University Press.

[7] Cerny, P.G. 1997. "Paradoxes of the Competition State: The Dynamics of Political Globalization." *Government and Opposition* 32, no. 2, pp. 251–74.

[8] Reich, S. 1998. *What Is Globalization?: Four Possible Answers*, 261 vols. Helen Kellogg Institute for International Studies. University of Notre Dame. IN, USA.

[9] Lerche C.O., III. 1998. "The Conflicts of Globalization." *International Journal of Peace Studies* 3, no. 1, pp. 47–66.

[10] Holm, H.H., and G. Sørensen. 1995. *Whose World Order?: Uneven Globalization and the End of the Cold War*. Westview Pr. CO, USA.

[11] Jones, R.B. 2013. *Globalisation and Interdependence in the International Political Economy: Rhetoric and Reality*. Bloomsbury Publishing. London, UK.

[12] Carnoy, M., M. Castells, S. Cohen, and F.H. Cardoso. 1993. *The New Global Economy in the Informational Age: Reflections on Our Changing World*. Penn State Press. PA, USA

[13] Harvey, D. 1999. "Time-Space Compression and the Postmodern Condition." *Modernity: Critical Concepts* 4, pp. 98–118.

[14] Giddens, A. 1990. "Thee Consequences of Modernity Cambridge." *Polity* 53, no. 83, pp. 245–60.

[15] Giddens, A. 2000. *Runaway World: How Globalization is Reshaping Our Lives*. New York: Routledge.

[16] Gilpin, R. 2000. *The Challenge of Global Capitalism*. Princeton, NJ: Princeton University Press.

[17] Jarvis, D.S. 2007. "Risk, Globalisation and the State: A Critical Appraisal of Ulrich Beck and the World Risk Society Thesis." *Global Society* 21, no. 1, pp. 23–46.

[18] Grevi, G., D. Keohane, B. Lee, and P. Lewis. 2013. *Empowering Europe's Future: Governance, Power, and Options for the EU in a Changing World*. the European Union. Paris, France.

[19] World Trade Organization. 2023. World Trade Statistical Review 2023.

[20] UNCTAD. 2023. South-South Trade Trends and Future Outlook.

[21] OECD. 2023. Trade in Value Added (TiVA) database.

[22] Baldwin, R.E., and P. Martin. 1999. *Two Waves of Globalisation: Superficial Similarities, Fundamental Differences (No. w6904)*. National Bureau of Economic Research.

[23] IMF. 2023. World Economic Outlook.

[24] World Bank. 2023. World Development Indicators.

[25] PwC. 2023. The World in 2050: The Long View.

[26] Bivens, J. 2007. "Globalization, American wages, and inequality." The Past, Present, and Future, Economic Policy Institute. Working Paper, 279.

[27] Benvenisti, E., and G. Nolte. 2004. *The Welfare State, Globalization, and International Law*. Springer Science & Business Media. Berlin, Germany.

[28] Stiglitz, J.E. 2003. *The Roaring Nineties: A New History of the World's Most Prosperous Decade*. New York, NY: W.W. Norton & Company.

CHAPTER 3

Transformation of Cultural Values and Attitudes

Moving from Traditional to Modern/ Postmodern Cultural Values

In the past four decades, cultural values have undergone profound transformations, driven by a confluence of factors such as economic development, technological advancement, globalization, and evolving social structures [1, 2]. These cultural shifts are most prominently observed in Western and European societies but have also significantly influenced other regions across the world. For example, the legalization of same-sex marriage in the Netherlands (2001), Spain (2005), and Taiwan (2019) reflects the global diffusion of secular and inclusive values [3]. Similarly, the expansion of women's participation in higher education and the workforce in South Korea and the United Arab Emirates (UAE) demonstrates the erosion of traditional gender roles.

This process of cultural change is part of the broader modernization process, wherein societies transition from traditional values—rooted in religion, hierarchy, and community cohesion—to modern values that prioritize rationality, individual rights, and personal freedom. According to Inglehart [8], modernization leads to a shift from traditional/ religious and survival-oriented values to secular/rational and self-expression values, characterized by the declining influence of religion and authoritarianism, the rise of individualism, gender equality, and an increasing emphasis on human rights, environmental sustainability, and self-expression [4].

Modernization theorists, such as Bell [5, 6], Huntington [7], and Inglehart [8], argue that there is a strong link between socioeconomic development and cultural change. As societies progress economically and politically through industrialization and bureaucratization, they undergo processes such as urbanization and occupational differentiation, which contribute to greater societal complexity [9]. These transformations lead to cultural shifts, including the rise of individualism, gender egalitarianism, changing attitudes toward authority, declining fertility rates, and the adoption of democratic governance and broader political participation [8]. For example, Japan's declining birth rate and the expansion of youth political participation in Chile after democratic reforms in the 1990s reflect these patterns.

Inglehart [8] explains cultural modernization through two primary dimensions:

1. Traditional Versus Secular-Rational Values
   Religiosity, deference to authority, strong family bonds, and adherence to absolute moral standards characterize traditional societies. These societies often reject practices such as divorce, abortion, euthanasia, and homosexuality. Saudi Arabia's historical prohibition of cinemas and restrictions on women's public roles before the reforms of the late 2010s illustrate this value orientation. In contrast, secular–rational societies embrace secularism, rationality, and tolerance for diverse lifestyles, as seen in Sweden's high rates of religious nonaffiliation and progressive social policies [10].

2. Survival Versus Self-Expression Values
   Societies emphasizing survival values prioritize materialistic and security-oriented concerns, display lower levels of subjective well-being, and tend to be intolerant of outgroups [1]. For instance, in many low-income or politically unstable countries, such as Afghanistan or Sudan, social attitudes remain cautious toward rapid social liberalization [11]. In contrast, self-expression value-oriented societies emphasize subjective well-being, freedom of expression, empowerment, imagination, and quality of life—traits visible in Denmark's emphasis on work–life balance, creative industries, and strong protections for freedom of speech.

Empirical studies show that societies with a predominantly agricultural workforce tend to uphold traditional values. At the same time, those with a higher proportion of industrial and service-sector workers are more likely to adopt secular–rational and self-expression values [12] (Figure 3.1). The rapid industrialization and subsequent social liberalization in Ireland—from a deeply Catholic, agrarian society in the mid-20th century to a socially progressive, service-based economy in the 21st century—illustrate this trajectory. The move from industrial to postindustrial societies amplifies self-expression values, as seen in the tech-driven cultures of Silicon Valley and other innovation hubs.

Western and European societies have been at the forefront of these cultural changes, but modernization's influence is increasingly global. While regional differences persist—such as the continued strength of traditionalism in parts of Africa, the Middle East, and South Asia—the overall trend points toward expanding modern cultural values, driven by globalization and generational change. The spread of Internet access, cross-cultural media consumption (e.g., K-pop in Latin America, American films in Africa), and international migration further accelerates this value transformation [13].

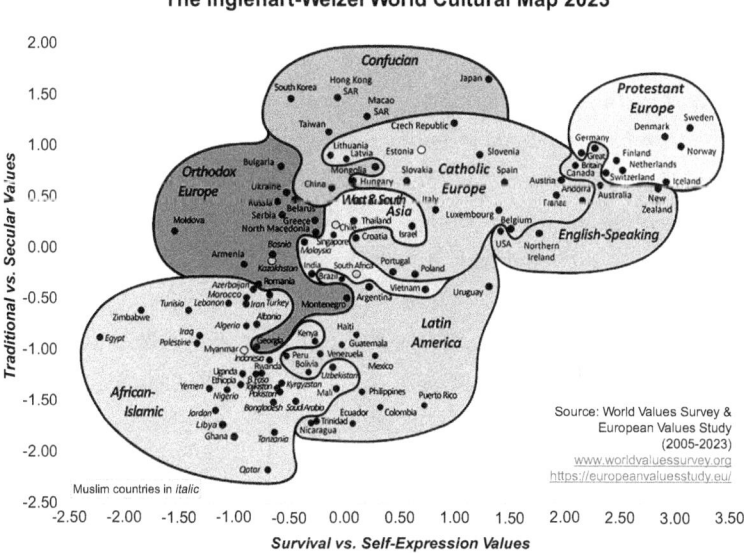

Figure 3.1 *The cultural modernization across the world*

Declining Religious Influence in the West and Across the World

A significant trend in cultural transformation is the declining importance of religiosity in many Western societies. In 1970, approximately 90 percent of Western Europeans were identified as Christians. Today, however, fewer than half of the population in countries such as Sweden, the Netherlands, and the United Kingdom consider themselves religious, reflecting a marked rise in secularization. Church attendance in the Netherlands has dropped sharply—from around 50 percent in the 1960s to less than 10 percent today. Similarly, in France, only about 32 percent of the population regard religion as a critical aspect of their lives, signaling a profound cultural shift. This decline in religious adherence coincides with legislative changes, including the widespread legalization of same-sex marriage, abortion, and euthanasia across Europe. These developments underscore a broader replacement of religious moral frameworks with secular and expressive values that increasingly shape societal norms and policies.

Beyond the West, the pace and extent of secularization vary significantly by region. In Czechia, over 70 percent of the population identifies as having no religion, making it one of the most secular countries globally [14]. Estonia exhibits similar trends, with fewer than 20 percent of people reporting religious belief or practice [15]. In Russia, while official Orthodoxy has reemerged in public discourse, regular church attendance remains low. Fewer than 10 percent of Russians attend services weekly, particularly among urban youth [15].

In East Asia, religiosity has traditionally been less institutionalized and more syncretic, yet recent decades have revealed a clear trend toward secularization. Japan is widely regarded as one of the most secular nations in the world. According to the Pew Research Center [16], only about 10–20 percent of Japanese adults consider religion to be vital in their lives. In South Korea, despite the expansion of Christianity during the 20th century, recent surveys indicate declining church attendance and increasing nonaffiliation among younger generations. According to the 2021 Korean census, over 60 percent of the population reports no religious affiliation [17].

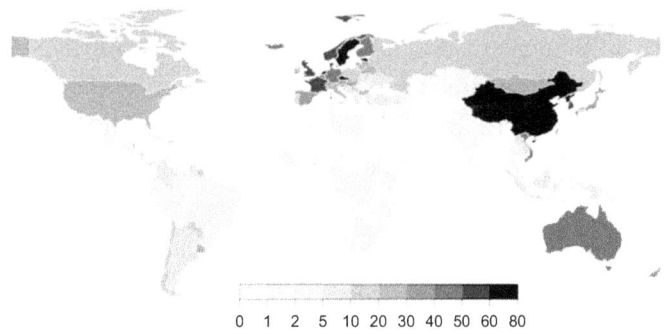

Figure 3.2 The percentage of atheism in 2020

Source: [37]

Traditionally Catholic, Latin America is undergoing significant religious transformation, marked by both the decline of Catholicism and the rise of secularism. In Uruguay, over 40 percent of the population identifies as religiously unaffiliated. In Chile and Argentina, secularism is also gaining traction, particularly among the youth [16].

Sub-Saharan Africa and South Asia remain highly religious overall, but early signs of secular value shifts are becoming visible. Urban youth in countries such as South Africa, Nigeria, and India increasingly embrace individualized spiritual practices and show declining adherence to institutional religion. In Kenya, data from Afrobarometer reveal a modest but notable generational gap in religious intensity, especially in Nairobi and other urban centers [11].

While secularization remains most prominent in Western societies, growing evidence from Latin America, East Asia, Oceania, and parts of Eastern Europe and Africa indicates that similar patterns are taking hold elsewhere. These shifts align with Inglehart's theory that rising existential security, increased education, and the spread of postmaterialist values contribute to the declining role of religion in modern societies [19] (Figure 3.2).

The Rise of Individualism and Gender Equality

One of the most defining features of contemporary cultural change is the growing emphasis on individual rights, personal autonomy, and freedom.

This transformation—reflected in both evolving personal values and institutional reforms—marks a decisive departure from traditional norms that prioritized conformity, respect for authority, and collective obligations. Longitudinal data from the World Values Survey (WVS) show that this global trend is especially pronounced in advanced industrialized societies, particularly in Western Europe, North America, and parts of East Asia [12]. Countries such as Sweden, the Netherlands, Canada, and the United States consistently score high on indicators of individualism, a pattern strongly correlated with high levels of economic development, educational attainment, and democratic governance [19].

A central marker of this cultural shift is the transformation of family structures. Historically, families functioned as tightly bound social units that emphasized duty, shared responsibilities, and intergenerational obligations. Marriage was widely regarded as a permanent institution, with social norms often limiting personal choice. Today, WVS data indicate growing acceptance of diverse family arrangements, including single-parent households, cohabitation without marriage, voluntary childlessness, and same-sex partnerships [20]. In countries such as Sweden and the Netherlands, these alternative forms are not only socially normalized but also supported by progressive policies, such as legal recognition of same-sex unions and generous parental leave [21]. Such developments underscore the rising primacy of individual agency and the gradual decline of collective, role-based norms in intimate and family life (Figure 3.3).

The rise of individualism is closely intertwined with the advancement of gender equality. Ronald Inglehart's theory of cultural change posits that as societies transition from survival values to self-expression values, they adopt more egalitarian views on gender roles [2]. This progression is visible in the growing participation of women across social, political, and economic domains. Since the 1970s, women's labor force participation has risen steadily, with several European countries now reporting rates above 70 percent. This shift reflects not only structural economic changes but also a redefinition of gender norms consistent with broader individualistic values.

Nordic countries—particularly Sweden, Norway, and Iceland—have emerged as global leaders in gender equality, implementing comprehensive family and labor policies that promote gender balance. These include generous parental leave, subsidized child care, and affirmative action measures designed to increase women's representation in leadership roles [22]. Such policies are grounded in cultural frameworks that prioritize autonomy, fairness, and personal fulfillment, reinforcing the link between self-expression values and progressive gender norms [12].

Support for gender equality in self-expression societies extends beyond the workplace, encompassing education, political representation, and legal reform. Across many of these nations, women's representation in parliaments, executive positions, and higher education has grown substantially. Generational data further reveal that younger cohorts—especially in countries scoring high on self-expression values—express stronger endorsement of gender equality and expect parity across all spheres of public and private life [19].

The rise of individualism and gender equality thus represents a profound cultural transformation, shaped by modernization, democratization, and shifting moral priorities. As societies move away from rigid hierarchies and traditional social structures, they are redefining the boundaries of identity, intimacy, and civic life. These changes carry significant long-term implications—not only for the expansion of personal freedoms but also for the institutional underpinnings of contemporary democratic societies.

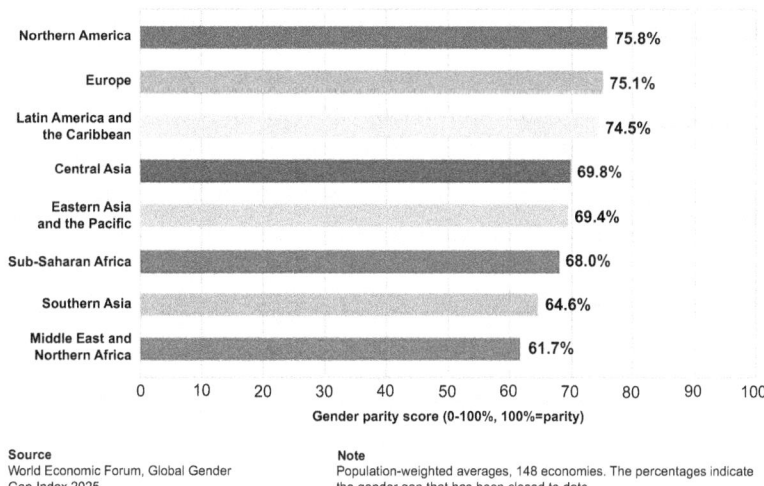

Source
World Economic Forum, Global Gender Gap Index 2025.

Note
Population-weighted averages, 148 economies. The percentages indicate the gender gap that has been closed to date.

Figure 3.3 Gender gap closed to date, by region

Migration, Multiculturalism, and Social Fragmentation

Less developed economies tend to be characterized by firm adherence to traditional, religious, and familial values, pronounced gender disparities, collectivist social norms, and higher fertility rates. These features contribute to the production of large numbers of migrants and young laborers seeking opportunities abroad [2]. In contrast, more developed nations are defined by modern, secular, and individualistic values, higher levels of gender equality, and declining birth rates—factors that make them natural destinations for economic migrants.

Over the past three decades, the intensification of globalization—driven by digitalization, enhanced communication networks, and improved transportation—has facilitated large-scale migration from developing to developed countries. As a result, many Western nations have become increasingly diverse across ethnic, racial, cultural, linguistic, and religious lines. For example, France reports that more than 10 percent of its population is composed of foreign nationals, nearly half of whom originate from Africa. In Germany, immigration has profoundly shaped demographics, with over 1 million migrants arriving in 2016 and first-generation immigrants accounting for more than 17 percent of the population by 2021 [23]. This percentage is projected to rise further by 2025 due to ongoing migration and refugee inflows.

Urban centers in Europe and North America—such as London, Paris, Frankfurt, Brussels, Toronto, New York, Los Angeles, and Chicago—have evolved into highly diverse metropolitan regions. Toronto, for example, is home to a population in which over 51 percent were born outside of Canada [24]. According to the U.S. Census Bureau (2020), more than 45 million migrants resided in the United States, representing approximately 14 percent of the population. By 2025, this figure is expected to grow further due to the sustained demand for skilled and unskilled labor. The U.S.–Mexico border has become a focal point of this demographic shift, with over 1.6 million migrant encounters recorded in fiscal year 2021, and a daily influx exceeding 12,000 migrants by 2023 [25].

Implications of Migration and Diversity

The rising diversity in cities across North America and Europe has wide-ranging implications. On one hand, immigration contributes to economic dynamism, cultural enrichment, and demographic vitality. On the other hand, it also presents significant challenges related to integration, social cohesion, and equitable resource distribution.

Cultural and linguistic gaps between migrants and host populations can hinder integration. Many migrants face unemployment, discrimination, and social marginalization, often living in ethnic enclaves that reinforce their separation from mainstream society. This marginalization is exacerbated when migrants neither fully retain their native culture nor fully assimilate into the host culture—an in-between state that leads to identity dislocation [26]. Migrants frequently report experiencing exclusion due to race, religion, language, or socioeconomic status, especially when host societies exhibit low tolerance for cultural differences. The greater the cultural distance between the host and migrant cultures, the higher the risk of alienation.

In extreme cases, lack of integration and rising frustration among marginalized groups can lead to social unrest. Notable examples include the riots in Paris in 2005 and 2023 and in London in 2011, which involved the burning of vehicles, attacks on public buildings, and looting. These events reveal underlying tensions between ethnoreligious minorities and the broader national community.

National approaches to cultural diversity vary widely. Canada embraces official multiculturalism, promoting linguistic and cultural pluralism. In contrast, countries like France emphasize a unitary national identity based on cultural and linguistic homogeneity, rooted in the republican ideal of "liberté, égalité, fraternité" [27]. Others take more coercive approaches, attempting to assimilate minority populations through education, language policies, or symbolic national integration [28].

While multiculturalism can promote cross-cultural understanding and enrich societies, it may also produce social fragmentation if cultural integration is weak or imbalanced. Cultural conflicts can arise when dominant groups impose their values on minorities or when divergent

Figure 3.4 Diversity could become a source of social conflict: French police confronting a woman on a beach as part of a controversial ban on the burkini in 2016

Source: [38]

views on gender roles, religious practice, or ethics clash within the public sphere. In addition, competition over jobs, housing, education, and political representation can create tension between cultural groups living in proximity (Figure 3.4).

Diversity, Equity, and Inclusion in the Era of Globalization

In today's interconnected world, diversity, equity, and inclusion (DEI) have moved from the periphery of national governance and public policy to the center of corporate strategy. For multinational corporations (MNCs), diversity is no longer merely an ethical imperative; it is increasingly recognized as a strategic asset that enhances competitiveness, innovation, and market adaptability [29].

As firms expand into culturally heterogeneous markets, a diverse workforce becomes essential for understanding local consumer preferences, cultural norms, and behavioral patterns. Employing individuals from varied ethnic, cultural, linguistic, and national backgrounds enables organizations to localize products and services more effectively, thereby improving global responsiveness and customer engagement [30].

Beyond market alignment, diversity strengthens innovation and problem-solving capacity. Empirical evidence shows that heterogeneous teams—drawing on varied perspectives, life experiences, and cognitive approaches—are more likely to generate creative solutions [31]. This innovative capacity provides advantages in product development, marketing, and organizational agility, particularly in competitive and rapidly changing markets.

Inclusivity in the Corporate Context

Inclusivity refers to deliberate efforts to ensure that employees from all backgrounds are respected, supported, and empowered to contribute meaningfully to organizational goals. Inclusive organizations go beyond diverse hiring practices to cultivate environments characterized by psychological safety, equitable opportunity, and cultural sensitivity [32]. Initiatives may include mentorship programs, inclusive leadership training, flexible work arrangements, and accommodations for religious and cultural practices.

However, inclusivity can produce unintended effects when pursued to ideological extremes. Some advocates of radical inclusivity challenge long-standing organizational norms—such as standardized testing, formal performance evaluations, punctuality, and financial performance metrics—arguing that these perpetuate systemic bias [33]. While these critiques highlight structural inequities, uncritical rejection of performance standards risks undermining meritocracy, operational efficiency, and clarity in decision making, potentially diminishing overall effectiveness.

Affirmative Action

Affirmative action, or positive discrimination, remains a contested tool for advancing workplace diversity. Proponents argue that it addresses historical injustices, corrects systemic underrepresentation, and levels the playing field for marginalized communities. Critics caution that poorly designed programs can reduce efficiency, generate resentment, and stigmatize beneficiaries by raising doubts about their accomplishments [34]. If mismanaged, such measures may also foster identity-based divisions, undermining workplace cohesion and trust.

The DEI in Practice

Alongside multiculturalism, DEI frameworks have gained prominence across both public and private institutions, particularly in the United States and Western Europe. These approaches aim to address structural inequities and foster inclusive environments through targeted interventions:

Diversity: Inclusion of individuals from varied demographic backgrounds, including race, ethnicity, gender, religion, disability, sexual orientation, and socioeconomic status.

Equity: Adapting systems and policies to address systemic barriers and ensure equal access to opportunities and resources.

Inclusion: Creating environments where all individuals feel valued, respected, and empowered to contribute fully.

Typical DEI programs include implicit bias training, employee resource groups, inclusive leadership initiatives, equitable promotion pathways, and cultural accommodations. Advocates contend that such measures enhance fairness, workplace culture, and global competitiveness. However, critics question their tangible impact, noting that empirical evidence linking DEI investment to improved performance remains limited [35].

Cultural Shifts and Public Attitudes

The rise of DEI reflects a broader cultural transformation. Public attitudes toward race, ethnicity, gender identity, and sexual orientation have shifted significantly in recent decades. For example, U.S. support for same-sex marriage grew from 35 percent in 1990 to over 70 percent by 2023 [36]. In Europe, approval rates are even higher—80 percent in Spain and 85 percent in Sweden. These shifts have translated into policy changes, including antidiscrimination laws, legalized same-sex unions, and protections for sexual and gender minorities.

Political representation has also diversified. Leaders such as Sanna Marin, Finland's former prime minister, and Leo Varadkar, Ireland's former Taoiseach—an openly gay leader of Indian heritage—symbolize the growing acceptance of diverse identities in positions of power. At the supranational level, the EU actively promotes inclusivity, refugee integration, and antidiscrimination measures.

Cultural change is further evident in media representation, education reform, and generational attitudes. Millennials and Generation Z, in particular, show more substantial support for diversity and inclusivity than older cohorts and expect institutions to embody these values. This generational shift suggests that multiculturalism and DEI principles will remain deeply embedded in the social, political, and economic fabric of the coming decades.

References

[1] Inglehart, R., and W.E. Baker. 2000. "Modernization, Cultural Change, and the Persistence of Traditional Values." *American Sociological Review* 65, no. 1, pp. 19–51.

[2] Norris, P., and R. Inglehart. 2019. *Cultural Backlash: Trump, Brexit, and Authoritarian Populism*. Cambridge University Press.

[3] Kollman, K. 2016. "The Same-Sex Unions Revolution in Western Democracies: International Norms and Domestic Policy Change." In *The Same-Sex Unions Revolution in Western Democracies*. Manchester University Press.

[4] Inglehart, R.F., M. Basanez, and A. Moreno. 1998. *Human Values and Beliefs: A Cross-Cultural Sourcebook*. University of Michigan Press.

[5] Bell, D. 1976. *The Cultural Contradictions of Capitalism*. New York, NY: Basic Books.

[6] Bell, D. 1973. The Coming of Post-Industrial Society. New York: Basic Books.

[7] Huntington, S.P. (1968). Political Order in Changing Societies. New Haven, CT: Yale University Press.

[8] Inglehart, R.F. (1997), *Modernization and Post-Modernization: Cultural, Economic and Political Change in 43 Societies*. Princeton, NJ: Princeton University Press.

[9] Bendix, R. 1974. "Inequality and Social Structure: A Comparison of Marx and Weber." *American Sociological Review* 39, no. 2, pp. 149–161.

[10] Pettersson, T., and Y. Esmer. 2008. *Changing Values, Persisting Cultures: Case Studies in Value Change*, 12 vol. Brill.

[11] World Value Survey. 2022. https://www.worldvaluessurvey.org/WVSNews ShowMore.jsp?evYEAR=2022&evMONTH=-1

[12] Welzel, C., and R. Inglehart. 2005. "Liberalism, Postmaterialism, and the Growth of Freedom." *International Review of Sociology* 15, no. 1, pp. 81–108.

[13] Castells, M. 2011. The Power of Identity, 14 vol. John Wiley & Sons.

[14] European Value Survey. https://europeanvaluesstudy.eu/

[15] Kramer, S., C. Hackett, and Beveridge, K. 2022. "Modeling the future of religion in America." Pew Research Center, 13.

[16] Pew Research Center. 2017. https://www.pewresearch.org/short-reads/2017/12/26/17-striking-findings-from-2017/

[17] Statistics Korea. 2021. https://kostat.go.kr/anse/

[18] https://www.pewresearch.org/internet/2014/02/11/main-report-30/

[19] Inglehart, R. 2018. *Culture Shift in Advanced Industrial Society*. Princeton University Press.

[20] Inglehart, R. 2021. *Religion's Sudden Decline: What's Causing it, and What Comes Next?*. Oxford University Press.

[21] Esping-Andersen, G. 2009. *Incomplete Revolution: Adapting Welfare States to Women's New Roles*. Polity.

[22] Stefán, C.I. 2023. "The World Economic Forum." In *The Palgrave Handbook of Non-State Actors in East-West Relations*, 1–13. Cham: Springer International Publishing.

[23] The Migration Report. 2021. https://www.bamf.de/SharedDocs/Anlagen/EN/Forschung/Migrationsberichte/migrationsbericht-2021.html?nn=447198

[24] A snapshot of Toronto: 51% of residents were born outside Canada, Vital Signs Report finds. http://news.nationalpost.com/toronto/a-snapshot-of-toronto-51-of-residents-were-born-outside-canada-vital-signs-report-finds

[25] Harris, C. 2021. The 2020 Census.

[26] Cesari, J. 2005. When Islam and Democracy Meet: Muslims in Europe and in the United States. Palgrave Macmillan.

[27] Conversi, D. 2002. *The Basques, the Catalans and Spain: Alternative Routes to Nationalist Mobilisation*. University of Nevada Press.

[28] https://theguardian.com/world/2016/aug/24

[29] Meyer, K.E., R. Mudambi, and R. Narula. 2011. Multinational Enterprises and Local Contexts: The Opportunities and Challenges of Multiple Embeddedness. *Journal of Management Studies* 48, no. 2, pp. 235–252.

[30] Yeganeh, H. 2022. "A Cross-National Investigation into the Effects of Religion on Gender Equality." *International Journal of Sociology and Social Policy* 42, no. 5/6, pp. 434–454.

[31] Østergaard, C. R., B. Timmermans, and K. Kristinsson. 2011. "Does a Different View Create Something New? The Effect of Employee Diversity on Innovation." *Research Policy* 40, no. 3, pp. 500–509.

[32] Shore, L.M., J.N. Cleveland, and D. Sanchez. 2018. "Inclusive Workplaces: A Review and Model." *Human Resource Management Review* 28, no. 2, pp. 176–189.

[33] Sensoy, Ö., and R. DiAngelo. 2017. "We Are All for Diversity, but...": How Faculty Hiring Committees Reproduce Whiteness and Practical Suggestions for How They Can Change." *Harvard Educational Review* 87, no. 4, pp. 557–580.

[34] Heilman, M.E. 2012. "Gender Stereotypes and Workplace Bias." *Research in organizational Behavior* 32, pp. 113–135.

[35] Kalev, A., F. Dobbin, and E. Kelly. 2006. "Best Practices or Best Guesses? Assessing the Efficacy of Corporate Affirmative Action and Diversity Policies." *American Sociological Review* 71, no. 4, pp. 589–617.

[36] Liu, J. 2009. Public Opinion on Same-Sex Marriage in the US (2009).

[37] https://colinmathers.com/2020/09/05/religiosity-and-atheism-in-2020/

[38] https://www.theguardian.com/world/2016/aug/24/french-police-make-woman-remove-burkini-on-nice-beach

CHAPTER 4

The Salient Features of Contemporary Global Culture

The Disembedment of Time and Space

Over the past two decades, globalization and technological innovation have profoundly altered our perception of time and space. Historically, human interaction, economic activity, and communication were constrained by geographic distance and temporal limits. With the advent of digital technologies and increasingly interconnected global markets, these constraints have been eroded. Anthony Giddens (1991) describes this phenomenon as the disembedding of time and space—the diminishing relevance of physical and temporal boundaries in an era shaped by globalization, digitalization, and digital capitalism [1].

From the outset, businesses and technologies have sought to dismantle spatial and temporal barriers to enhance productivity and returns on investment [2, 3]. The global economy now operates on a continuous 24/7 cycle, enabling real-time transactions and the coordination of complex supply chains across multiple time zones. The historic dominance of traditional economic hubs—metropolitan cities and financial centers—is being challenged as advances in communication and information technology enable remote work and decentralized organizational structures.

Where physical presence was once essential for business, education, or social engagement, digital communication has transformed these interactions. Multinational corporations now manage operations across continents; e-commerce platforms serve customers worldwide without physical stores; and businesses increasingly rely on virtual, outsourced teams that operate independently of time zones.

One of the most profound changes is the redefinition of the workplace. Stable, location-based structures are giving way to flexible, project-oriented work arrangements [4]. The rise of part-time, contract-based, and gig employment models reflects a broader shift away from centralized offices. This trend reduces the economic primacy of cities while enabling skilled workers in rural or remote areas to participate in global labor markets. By decoupling work from physical offices, firms gain access to wider talent pools and reduce costs, while digital platforms ensure seamless coordination across time zones. The modern workplace increasingly functions as a "nonspace"—a setting in which traditional hierarchies and institutional dependencies are diminished [5].

The dislocation of time and space extends beyond labor markets, reshaping education, entertainment, and social interaction [3]. Virtual learning platforms have replaced traditional classrooms, making education accessible regardless of location. Streaming services have freed entertainment from fixed schedules, offering on-demand access to global content. E-commerce enables seamless cross-border transactions without physical storefronts. Social media platforms facilitate the creation of communities across vast distances, often supplanting local relationships with digital connections that function as global commons.

The consequences are far-reaching. Remote work and outsourcing have restructured labor markets, enabling companies such as Amazon and Google to leverage global workforces for uninterrupted service. Financial systems are being transformed as decentralized financial technologies and cryptocurrencies—such as Bitcoin and Ethereum—offer borderless, round-the-clock transactions, challenging the time-bound operations of traditional banks. In health care, telemedicine platforms connect patients with physicians worldwide, expanding access and reducing reliance on in-person consultations. Culturally, the global dissemination of products such as Korean pop music (K-pop) through YouTube and TikTok demonstrates how digital media transcend national boundaries, reshaping consumption patterns and cultural identities.

Globalization and digitalization have redefined the meaning of time and space, dismantling constraints that once shaped economic, educational, and cultural life. The shift toward a world less bound by location and time has produced new economic structures, labor models, and digital practices that are transforming daily life. While these developments bring unprecedented efficiency and opportunity, they also raise pressing challenges—job insecurity, digital dependency, and the erosion of localized social networks. Addressing these issues will require sustained research and carefully designed policies as the transformation of human experience under globalization continues to accelerate.

Temporal Acceleration

Over the past two decades, globalization, digitalization, and technological innovation have produced an unprecedented acceleration of time across economic, social, and cultural domains. In capitalist systems, time has increasingly become a critical factor of production and a valuable economic asset. The rapid circulation of capital, combined with advances in communication and information technologies, has intensified the tempo of business operations, social interactions, and daily life [2, 6]. The German philosopher Hartmut Rosa (2003) describes this phenomenon as the compression of the present—a condition in which social and cultural transformations unfold at an ever-increasing pace. This acceleration now permeates nearly every aspect of human life, including politics, labor, relationships, and leisure [7] (Figure 4.1).

Rosa (2003) identifies three interrelated forms of temporal acceleration. Technological acceleration refers to the rapid development of transportation, communication, and production systems, enabling faster transactions, interactions, and data processing. Social acceleration describes the increasing pace at which norms, values, and cultural trends evolve, reshaping personal relationships, social expectations, and institutional frameworks. The acceleration of the pace of life captures the growing perception of time as a scarce resource, often leading to heightened stress, time pressure, and a constant sense of urgency [7].

Technological innovation is the primary driver of this transformation. Advances in microcomputing—marked by exponential increases in processing power, storage capacity, and affordability—have dramatically shortened the time required to access, process, and share information. Butters' Law observes that optical fiber data transmission capacity doubles approximately every nine months, reflecting the accelerating efficiency of digital infrastructure [8]. The effects are visible in human behavior: a Microsoft study reported that the average attention span fell from 12 seconds in 2000 to 8 seconds in 2012, underscoring the cognitive impact of digital saturation [9]. The rise of instant messaging, email, and social media has fostered expectations of near-instantaneous responses, reshaping both professional workflows and personal exchanges.

Economically, temporal acceleration has transformed corporate strategies and organizational structures. Businesses must respond rapidly to shifting market conditions, adapt quickly to consumer demands, and exploit short-lived opportunities to remain competitive. Companies such as Amazon have built their business models around speed—integrating digital logistics and e-commerce to normalize instant gratification and rapid delivery. This environment prioritizes speed over stability, shortens production cycles, and increases reliance on agile business models. The modern workplace now demands multitasking, constant connectivity, and shorter deadlines. At the same time, the gig economy—exemplified by platforms such as Uber and TaskRabbit—illustrates the fluid yet unpredictable scheduling patterns that define contemporary labor.

Cultural consumption has also accelerated. Online shopping, one-click purchasing, and same-day delivery services have embedded instant access into consumer expectations. Streaming platforms such as Netflix and YouTube have replaced fixed broadcast schedules with on-demand content, while fast-fashion retailers such as Zara and Shein produce and distribute new collections at breakneck speed, reinforcing cycles of transient trends and disposability.

Social relationships have adapted to this faster tempo. Digital communication tools enable frequent contact but often at the cost of depth and emotional engagement. Online dating apps prioritize rapid judgments through swiping mechanisms, while social media encourages short-form, ephemeral content that reinforces the pressure to remain constantly visible and relevant.

Examples of temporal acceleration's influence are widespread. The Arab Spring (2011) and the #MeToo movement (2017) illustrate how digital activism can mobilize mass participation and produce rapid cultural and political changes. In labor markets, the gig economy demands immediate service fulfillment, keeping workers in a state of near-constant

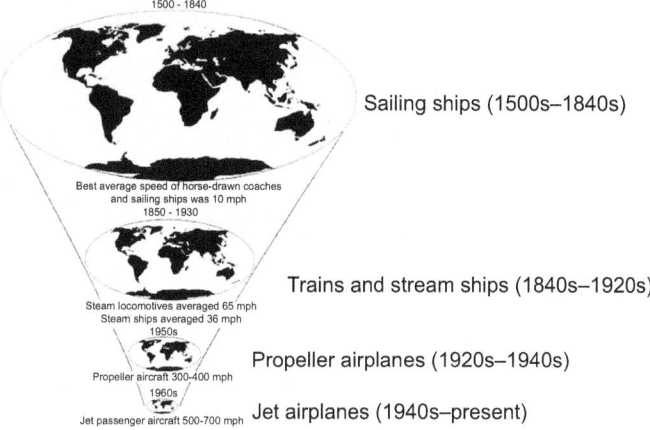

Figure 4.1 Time–space compression

Source: Harvey (1999) [2]

availability. Even leisure is affected: platforms such as TikTok and Instagram Reels have popularized short-form, easily consumable entertainment, reflecting a preference for speed over duration.

However, the effects are not uniformly positive. Acceleration can lead to stress, burnout, diminished attention spans, and more superficial social bonds. The rapid flow of information and trends may contribute to polarization, misinformation, and a reduced capacity for sustained reflection. While speed enhances efficiency, innovation, and global connectivity, it also raises concerns about well-being, social equity, and the quality of human interaction.

Short-Termism

Short-termism has become a defining by-product of temporal acceleration. The demand for instant responses—enabled by advanced communication technologies—has produced what Rosa (2003) describes as the *compression of the future into an extended present*. In this condition, the temporal boundaries that once separated the present from the future are increasingly blurred. As a result, decision making across economic, political, and social domains tends to favor immediate outcomes over long-term sustainability [7].

In the corporate world, short-termism drives organizations to prioritize quarterly performance and immediate shareholder returns over long-term strategy, innovation, and sustainability. This dynamic was starkly evident during the 2007–2008 financial crisis, when short-sighted, high-risk behavior destabilized financial institutions and global markets [10]. The excessive focus on near-term profits often leads firms to underinvest in R&D, delay the adoption of sustainable practices, and sacrifice employee well-being in the pursuit of financial efficiency [11].

Financial markets offer a clear illustration of this trend. High-frequency trading, powered by advanced computing and algorithmic platforms, executes transactions within milliseconds [12]. While such speed can generate rapid profits, it also fuels volatility and undermines the pursuit of long-term value creation. Similar pressures are visible in product development, particularly in technology sectors. Over the past two decades, the electronics industry has experienced sharply reduced product life cycles, with smartphones, laptops, and other devices frequently replaced within a few years due to rapid obsolescence and consumer demand for continual innovation [13].

Short-termism in politics manifests in policies aimed at securing immediate electoral gains or appeasing public opinion, often at the expense of long-term societal needs. This tendency encourages reactive measures over proactive reforms. Environmental policy is a prime example: governments frequently prioritize short-term economic growth—through industrial expansion or job creation—over long-term ecological sustainability. Such policies not only undermine climate change mitigation efforts but also impose environmental and economic costs on future generations.

The labor market reflects similar temporal compression. In traditional societies, occupations often spanned generations, with skills and roles passed down within families. Modernity shifted employment cycles to align with individual lifespans, but fragmented career trajectories increasingly define today's economy. Workers change jobs more frequently than ever; in 2022, the median tenure for U.S. wage and salary workers was only 4.1 years [14], indicating a growing culture of professional transience.

Family life has also adapted to the accelerated pace. Historically, families tended to be multigenerational and stable over lifetimes. In contrast, contemporary societies have seen rising divorce rates, increased remarriage, and diverse family arrangements. Marriage rates are declining globally, while divorce rates have risen in many Western nations [15]. These shifts mirror the short-term orientation evident in other social spheres, with intimate relationships often reflecting the same instability as careers and corporate strategies.

At the personal level, short-termism shapes daily decision making in consumption, health, relationships, and career planning. The preference for immediate gratification over long-term goals can lead to impulsive spending, substance abuse, overconsumption of digital content, and a tendency toward casual rather than enduring relationships. Technologies such as social media, online shopping, and streaming services reinforce this mindset, fostering habits that undermine financial stability, personal development, and emotional resilience.

Short-termism in the age of acceleration reflects a profound cultural and structural shift toward immediacy across public, private, and personal spheres. While this orientation can generate agility, responsiveness, and rapid innovation, it also erodes stability, undermines long-term planning, and weakens the commitments that once anchored social, economic, and political life. Addressing its consequences will require deliberate efforts to reintroduce long-term thinking into policy, corporate governance, and individual behavior.

Risk and Uncertainty

Globalization and digitalization have transformed the contemporary world by diminishing the relevance of national borders and compressing time and space. These processes have enabled unprecedented connectivity, economic integration, and technological advancement. However, they have also intensified economic, political, social, environmental, and technological vulnerabilities.

Sociologists such as Beck (1992, 2009) and Giddens (1991) conceptualize this as the emergence of a *risk society*, in which uncertainty and instability are defining features of modern life [1, 16]. Bauman (2013) adds to this by describing the *liquidity* of contemporary society—a fluid and unpredictable state in which traditional sources of stability, such as long-term employment, enduring personal relationships, and robust social institutions, have become increasingly fragile [17]. Beck (1992) further argues that globalization erodes the territorial sovereignty of nation-states, weakens governmental authority, and concentrates power in global financial markets and among international speculators—often at the expense of national economic stability [16].

Globalization generates multiple, interrelated forms of risk:

- Economic Risks: Unemployment, financial instability, market volatility, and currency fluctuations.
- Social Risks: Mass migration, identity crises, cultural tensions, and the erosion of traditional values.
- Security Risks: Terrorism, cyberattacks, industrial espionage, and breaches of privacy.
- Environmental Risks: Climate change, extreme weather events, rising sea levels, and biodiversity loss.
- Health Risks: The accelerated spread of diseases, as seen during the COVID-19 pandemic, is driven by global mobility and trade.

Global supply chains, a hallmark of economic globalization, are acutely vulnerable to disruption. Natural disasters, geopolitical conflicts, and financial crises can trigger cascading failures across industries and regions. The 2011 earthquake in Japan and the COVID-19 pandemic illustrate how localized disruptions can rapidly destabilize global production networks. Mitigating such risks requires robust international cooperation and coordinated crisis-response mechanisms.

Globalization's environmental implications are particularly severe in developing countries, where governments may relax environmental standards to attract foreign investment. This dynamic often results in pollution, resource depletion, and ecological degradation. Multinational corporations relocating to these jurisdictions may prioritize short-term profit over long-term sustainability, accelerating global environmental decline. Climate-related threats—such as intensified weather events and rising sea levels—represent existential challenges that demand urgent, globally coordinated mitigation strategies.

The diffusion of global cultural products—films, fashion, music, and consumer lifestyles—has contributed to cultural homogenization, raising concerns over the erosion of local traditions and identities. While cultural exchange can foster cosmopolitanism, it can also provoke resistance in more conservative societies, generating identity crises, social fragmentation, and even cultural conflict. This tension between traditional values and global cultural influences is increasingly evident in debates over language preservation, media representation, and societal norms.

Traditional risk assessment models—designed for localized and predictable threats—struggle to address the interconnected, transnational, and rapidly evolving risks of the globalized era. Effective risk governance now requires adaptive, cross-border strategies. Governments, corporations, and institutions must integrate advanced data analytics, scenario-based planning, and resilience-building into their decision-making processes. Such approaches can enhance preparedness, improve early-warning systems, and enable faster, more coordinated responses to complex, overlapping threats.

The age of globalization and digitalization has created a world of unprecedented opportunity and equally unprecedented risk. Navigating this environment demands a fundamental shift in how risks are perceived, assessed, and managed—one that embraces complexity, fosters international cooperation, and prioritizes resilience over short-term gain. Without such adaptation, the very forces driving global progress may also become the sources of its most profound instability.

The Culture of McDonaldization

Sociologist George Ritzer (2008) coined the term *McDonaldization* to describe the process by which the principles of the fast-food restaurant have come to dominate an ever-growing number of sectors in American society and, increasingly, across the world. Building on Max Weber's analysis of rationalization in modern bureaucracies, Ritzer identifies four central dimensions that define this phenomenon: efficiency, calculability, predictability, and control [18] (Table 4.1).

Efficiency refers to the most streamlined way of satisfying a need. In the fast-food model, it means moving from hunger to satiety as quickly as possible, with workers following predesigned and standardized processes. Calculability emphasizes quantitative measures such as portion size, price, and speed of service, often equating quantity with quality. Customers judge not only the cost of a meal but also the time it takes to obtain it. Predictability ensures that products and services remain consistent across locations and over time—so that a McDonald's customer in New York, Tokyo, or Paris can expect the same menu items, taste, and service. Control is exerted through nonhuman technologies, structured procedures, and environmental design—such as lines, limited menus, and uncomfortable seating—to regulate both employees and customers, encouraging quick, uniform, and efficient interactions.

Although the fast-food industry did not create society's demand for efficiency, it transformed it into a universal expectation. The principles of McDonaldization have spread far beyond food service into retail, education, health care, and entertainment. Department stores, shopping malls, and gas stations have adopted layouts and processes designed for speed and convenience. Universities increasingly use machine-graded tests to save time for faculty, emphasize quantifiable outputs such as grades and graduation rates, and standardize curricula and degree programs on a global scale. Hospitals organize patient care into standardized pathways, reducing the discretionary role of individual physicians. Streaming services such as Netflix and e-commerce platforms such as Amazon have revolutionized entertainment and shopping by providing instant access to content and products.

In a McDonaldized society, quantity often rivals—or even surpasses—quality in perceived value. In food service, the drive for mass production results in standardized but lower quality offerings. In education, emphasis shifts toward throughput—how many students graduate and their GPAs—rather than the depth or quality of learning. Businesses, hospitals, and municipalities are judged more by comparative rankings than by substantive outcomes. For workers, McDonaldization often means performing fragmented, repetitive tasks reminiscent of Fordist assembly-line production, leading to alienation and a loss of personal investment in one's work. In education, the quantification of student performance reduces learning to measurable outputs, while in entertainment and media, books, films, and television shows are continuously reviewed, ranked, and rated according to standardized criteria.

Nonhuman technology plays a key role in enforcing this system. Computers, automated processes, and pre-prepared goods control both employees and consumers. In fast-food restaurants, food is precooked, portioned, and seasoned to minimize worker discretion. In aviation, pilots increasingly rely on automated systems to guide aircraft between takeoff and landing. In supermarkets and hospitals, technological systems structure the entire customer or patient experience, reducing the role of human judgment. While such technologies enhance standardization and efficiency, they also erode craftsmanship, creativity, and personal interaction.

Ironically, the rationalization that underpins McDonaldization can produce inefficiencies and irrationalities. Excessive regulation and rigid processes can make services less responsive and strip them of genuine care. In education, the push for quick, inexpensive programs may compromise quality. By prioritizing quantity over quality, organizations risk alienating both customers and employees.

McDonaldization has thus become a defining cultural pattern of the modern world, shaping how goods and services are produced, delivered, and consumed. Its spread beyond the fast-food industry mirrors broader societal trends toward efficiency, standardization, and control. While it delivers convenience, predictability, and accessibility, it also brings significant costs: diminished quality, reduced human autonomy, and the erosion of meaningful social interactions.

Table 4.1 The four dimensions of McDonaldization

Dimension	Explanation	Examples
1. Efficiency	The optimal method for accomplishing a task	*The fastest way to get from being hungry to being full minimization of time*
2. Calculability	The quantification of objectives	*Quantity is translated into quality. Delivering a large amount of product to the customer in a short time is equivalent to providing high-quality products*
3. Predictability	The standardization and uniformity of products and services	*Always the same product, the same service, and the same task*
4. Control	Influencing the customers and employees via automation	*Limited menu, limited choice, and limited time for customers. Limited and repetitive tasks for employees*

The Posttruth Era: Instability of Meaning and Knowledge

The concept of posttruth has gained significant attention in recent years, reflecting a profound shift in how societies perceive and value facts and knowledge. While its philosophical roots extend back to the 19th century—most notably in Friedrich Nietzsche's rejection of positivist notions of objective truth, expressed in his assertion that "there are no facts, only interpretations" [19]—the term entered mainstream discourse in 2016 when Oxford Dictionaries selected it as their Word of the Year. The following year, Collins Dictionaries named "fake news" as its Word of the Year, signaling the increasing prominence of misinformation in public life [20].

Posttruth refers to situations in which objective facts exert less influence on public opinion than emotional appeals and personal beliefs. The prefix post implies a condition in which empirical evidence is overshadowed by subjective feelings [21]. It is the triumph of the visceral over the rational and the deceptively simple over the honestly complex [22]. Deception has not only become normalized but is often perceived as legitimate, blurring distinctions between truth and falsehood, honesty and dishonesty, reality and fiction.

A defining feature of the posttruth environment is the growing acceptance of relativistic viewpoints, where falsehoods are reframed as "alternative perspectives" or "legitimate opinions." While the expansion of diversity and inclusivity in public discourse has yielded positive outcomes, it has also facilitated the uncritical acceptance of contradictory claims—especially in multicultural, fragmented, and highly digitized communication spaces.

Drivers and Implications of the Posttruth Condition

Several interrelated forces have fueled the rise of posttruth dynamics in postindustrial societies. Globalization and digitalization have collapsed traditional boundaries of time and space, enabling information to circulate instantaneously—often without rigorous verification. Public trust in governments, media, and scientific authorities has eroded, fostering skepticism toward expert knowledge and official narratives. Jean Baudrillard's (2001) concept of hyperreality captures the idea that representations of reality increasingly eclipse reality itself, dissolving the boundary between truth and fiction [23]. Postmodern relativism has reinforced this trend by framing truth as context-dependent and fluid, weakening collective commitment to shared standards of truth.

Social media and digital platforms have amplified these tendencies by restructuring public discourse. Metrics such as likes, shares, and follower counts reward content that is viral, emotionally resonant, and sensational—regardless of accuracy. Algorithmic personalization intensifies confirmation bias, producing echo chambers that limit exposure to diverse perspectives. The proliferation of user-generated content further blurs the distinction between professional journalism and personal opinion, accelerating the spread of misinformation [24].

Real-world cases illustrate the instrumentalization of falsehoods in political life. U.S. Congressman George Santos fabricated extensive aspects of his biography yet secured election in 2022, remaining in office for nearly a year before expulsion. Former President Donald Trump's repeated claims that the 2020 election was stolen—despite clear evidence to the contrary—helped incite the January 6th Capitol attack and continue to polarize public opinion (Figure 4.2). In the United Kingdom, former Prime Minister Boris Johnson faced criticism for misleading statements regarding Brexit and the "Partygate" scandal during COVID-19 lockdowns. These examples underscore the diminished role of factual verification in political decision making and the capacity of misinformation to achieve political ends with limited accountability.

The erosion of trust and the proliferation of misinformation undermine the foundations of democratic governance. Citizens confronted with conflicting narratives may grow cynical, apathetic, or disillusioned, weakening civic participation. In such an environment, democratic institutions become more vulnerable to manipulation, and the integrity of elections, policymaking, and public deliberation is compromised. When objective truth loses authority, the legitimacy of democratic systems is fundamentally at risk.

The Posttruth Era and Its Implications for Business and Management

In an era where misinformation spreads rapidly and emotionally charged narratives shape public perception, businesses face heightened reputational and operational risks. False information can erode consumer loyalty and investor confidence, making transparency, fact-checking, and agile communication essential.

During crises, emotional narratives often dominate, challenging companies to respond authentically and promptly. Partnering with trusted third parties—experts, regulators, or credible influencers—can help reinforce credibility. Marketing strategies must balance emotional resonance with factual integrity, relying on ethical branding and honest storytelling to sustain trust.

Public skepticism toward corporate motives has intensified demands for accountability. Ethical leadership, transparent governance, and meaningful corporate social responsibility (CSR) initiatives are critical for rebuilding stakeholder confidence. Reliable decision making increasingly depends on verified data, requiring investment in accurate analytics, misinformation detection, and rigorous validation protocols.

Figure 4.2 Protesters storm the U.S. Capitol building during the January 6, 2021, riot that disrupted the certification of the 2020 presidential election results

As consumer trust in traditional advertising declines, authenticity becomes paramount. While influencer marketing, user-generated content, and social proof can enhance credibility, they must be deployed responsibly to avoid amplifying misinformation. Compliance with evolving digital regulations—on content, privacy, and advertising—is equally important for safeguarding brand integrity.

Financial markets are susceptible to misinformation, with rumors and false reports capable of destabilizing investor sentiment. Maintaining market confidence demands consistent financial disclosures and rapid-response mechanisms. Emerging threats such as deepfakes and synthetic media necessitate advanced monitoring tools, artificial intelligence (AI)-driven defenses, and collaboration with technology platforms to counter reputational attacks.

Finally, the volatility of the posttruth era complicates strategic forecasting. Businesses must adopt scenario planning, crisis preparedness, and organizational agility to remain resilient in an environment where public narratives can shift rapidly and unpredictably.

References

[1] Giddens, A. 1991. *The Consequences of Modernity*. Oxford: Blackwell.

[2] Harvey, D. 1999. "Time-Space Compression and the Postmodern Condition." *Modernity: Critical Concepts* 4, pp. 98–118.

[3] Huebener, P., S. O'Brien, T. Porter, L. Stockdale, and Y.R. Zhou. 2016. "Exploring the Intersection of Time and Globalization." *Globalizations* 13, no. 3, pp. 243–255.

[4] Berger, P.L., and S.P. Huntington, eds. 2003. *Many Globalizations: Cultural Diversity in the Contemporary World*. USA: Oxford University Press.

[5] Riain, S.Ó. 2006. "Time-Space Intensification: Karl Polanyi, the Double Movement, and Global Informational Capitalism." *Theory and Society* 35, no. 5–6, pp. 507–528.

[6] Martineau, J. 2017. "Culture in the Age of Acceleration, Hypermodernity, and Globalized Temporalities." *The Journal of Arts Management, Law, and Society* 47, no. 4, pp. 218–229.

[7] Rosa, H. 2003. "Social Acceleration: Ethical and Political Consequences of a Desynchronized High–Speed Society." *Constellations* 10, no. 1, pp. 3–33

[8] Robinson, G. 2000. "Speeding Net Traffic with Tiny Mirrors." *Electronic Engineering Times* 1133, pp. 30–31.

[9]   Lindner, E. 2012. *A Dignity Economy: Creating an Economy that Serves Human Dignity and Preserves Our Planet.* Dignity Press. https://adweek.com/digital/john-stevens-guest-post-decreasing-attention-spans/

[10] Dallas, L.L. 2011. "Short-Termism, the Financial Crisis, and Corporate Governance." *Journal of Corporation Law* 37, p. 265.

[11] Marginson, D., and L. McAulay. 2008. "Exploring the Debate on Short-Termism: A Theoretical and Empirical Analysis." *Strategic Management Journal* 29, no. 3, pp. 273–292.

[12] Aitken, M., F. Harris, and T. McInish. 2007. "High-Frequency Trading: An Overview." *Australian Journal of Management* 32, no. 1, pp. 23–35.

[13] Brose, H.G. 2004. "An Introduction to a Culture of Non-Simultaneity?." *Time & Society* 13, no. 1, pp. 5–26.

[14] Bureau of Labor Statistics. 2022. *Employee Tenure Summary.* https://www.bls.gov/news.release/tenure.nr0.htm

[15] Ortiz-Ospina, E., and M. Roser. 2020. *Marriages and Divorces.* Our World in Data. https://ourworldindata.org/marriages-and-divorces

[16] Beck, U. 1992. *Risk Society: Towards a New Modernity*, 17 vols. Sage.

[17] Bauman, Z. 2013. *Liquid Modernity.* John Wiley & Sons.

[18] Ritzer, G. 2008. *The McDonaldization of Society 5.* Pine Forge Press.

[19] Allison, D.B. 1979. "Destruction/Deconstruction in the Text of Nietzsche." *Boundary* 2, pp. 197–222.

[20] Hainscho, T. 2023. "Calling the News Fake: The Underlying Claims About Truth in the Post-Truth Era." *Philosophy & Social Criticism* 49, no. 7, pp. 786–797.

[21] McIntyre, L. 2018. *Post-Truth.* MIT Press.

[22] d'Ancona, M. 2017. *Post-Truth: The New War on Truth and How to Fight Back.* Random House.

[23] Baudrillard, J. 2001. *Jean Baudrillard: Selected Writings.* Stanford University Press.

[24] Allcott, H., and M. Gentzkow. 2017. "Social Media and Fake News in the 2016 Election." *Journal of Economic Perspectives* 31, no. 2, pp. 211–236.

CHAPTER 5

The Rise of Wokeism

Wokeism

The term *woke* originates from African American Vernacular English (AAVE), where it initially denoted a heightened awareness of social and political injustices, particularly those affecting Black communities [1]. Historically, it was used as an adjective to describe individuals who were alert to systemic oppression and inequality. The Urban Dictionary once defined it as someone who is "aware of community issues." Over time, the expression evolved into exhortations to *"stay woke"*—a call for vigilance in recognizing and confronting forms of racial injustice, such as police violence and white supremacy.

Over the past decade, "woke" has expanded from its original racial justice roots into a broader cultural and ideological phenomenon known as *wokeism*. This term encapsulates a set of beliefs, attitudes, and practices centered on progressive ideals, particularly concerning identity politics, systemic inequality, and social justice. Wokeism promotes awareness of and responsiveness to issues such as racism, sexism, homophobia, and other forms of discrimination. At its core, it seeks to challenge and dismantle entrenched societal norms and structures that perpetuate exclusion and inequality [1, 2].

In practice, wokeism has been adopted widely across both public and private institutions, including government bodies, corporations, nonprofit organizations, educational institutions, and even the military [3, 4]. These institutions have embedded woke principles into internal operations—through inclusive hiring policies, employee training on diversity and equity, and performance metrics tied to representation—and have broadcast these commitments externally through branding, public relations campaigns, and marketing strategies. The technology, entertainment, and media sectors, in particular, have played a leading role in promoting woke values, as demonstrated by their public support for movements such as Black Lives Matter in 2020 and their active participation in LGBTQ+ Pride celebrations (Figure 5.1).

This phenomenon, sometimes termed *woke capitalism*, reflects a strategic alignment between corporate values and progressive social causes. Many U.S. tech firms have pledged financial support for racial justice initiatives, expanded diversity recruitment efforts, and adopted inclusive messaging in public communications [5, 6]. Enabled by global media platforms and digital networks, such efforts have increasingly become a way to enhance brand identity, attract socially conscious consumers, and maintain competitive advantage in a values-driven marketplace.

Wokeism has also gained traction within the governmental sphere. Since 2020, the Biden administration has actively championed policies aligned with woke priorities, including DEI; LGBTQ+ rights; environmental justice; and protections for marginalized communities. The administration has appointed a historically diverse cabinet, issued executive orders promoting racial and gender equity, and endorsed more inclusive immigration and education policies. It has also supported the public discourse around frameworks such as Critical Race Theory, signaling a governmental embrace of systemic analysis in addressing inequality and discrimination.

Despite its widespread influence, wokeism remains a contested concept. Critics argue that the term *woke* has been co-opted and politicized, often used pejoratively to describe individuals or institutions perceived as excessively politically correct or moralizing. This backlash has fueled cultural and political polarization, with detractors viewing wokeism as an overreach that undermines meritocratic principles and freedom of expression. As with many ideologically charged terms, the meaning and implications of wokeism vary across contexts and are subject to ongoing debate [7–9]. Nonetheless, wokeism persists as a powerful cultural force. Its influence extends beyond policy and branding, redefining how societies perceive power, identity, language, and justice. As such, it continues to shape discourse and institutional practices, particularly in Western societies, where questions of inclusion, equity, and historical accountability have become central to the public imagination.

Figure 5.1 Black Lives Matter movement was galvanized by the death of George Floyd in 2020

Changing Power Relations and Social Structures

A central dimension of wokeism lies in its critical engagement with power relations and social structures. Grounded in intellectual traditions such as Critical Theory, Intersectionality, Critical Race Theory, Feminism, and Postcolonial Theory, wokeism promotes an explicit commitment to social justice. This commitment involves confronting systemic inequalities—including racism, sexism, homophobia, and other forms of structural discrimination—that persist within societal institutions [1, 2,10].

Wokeism actively champions both equality and equity, particularly in the domains of race and gender. It emphasizes diversity and inclusion, supporting policies aimed at ensuring equitable representation across demographic groups. These measures may include blind recruitment processes, diversity benchmarks, and inclusive workplace initiatives designed to cultivate environments where all individuals are respected and valued [11, 12]. The broader political agenda associated with wokeism often supports systemic reform, such as criminal justice reform, expanded voting rights, and antidiscrimination legislation.

In education, wokeism seeks to redress disparities by advocating for policies that promote equal access and opportunities for students from all socioeconomic backgrounds. It further supports increased representation of historically marginalized groups within political institutions to ensure that legislative and policymaking bodies reflect the diversity of the broader population. Affirmative action is frequently endorsed within this framework as a mechanism to address the cumulative disadvantages imposed on certain groups by historical and institutional discrimination [13].

Moreover, wokeism calls for a critical self-examination of privilege and societal advantage. This issue includes recognizing one's position within social hierarchies and taking active steps to redress past injustices. Examples include advocating for reparations, revisiting public commemorations, and renaming institutions tied to colonialism, slavery, or other oppressive legacies [11, 12].

Language, Discourse, and Cultural Representation in Wokeism

A second core dimension of wokeism pertains to the role of language and discourse in shaping public consciousness and reinforcing or challenging systems of inequality. Drawing from Critical and Intersectionality Theory, proponents argue that language is never neutral—it reflects and sustains power dynamics embedded in society [10, 14, 15].

Accordingly, wokeism emphasizes the use of inclusive and culturally sensitive language that affirms the dignity of all individuals, particularly those from marginalized communities. It critiques linguistic expressions that perpetuate stereotypes or normalize discriminatory attitudes, promoting instead a discourse marked by political correctness and respect for difference [2]. One prominent example of this linguistic sensitivity is the critique of cultural appropriation—the adoption of cultural elements from historically marginalized groups by dominant groups without proper understanding or respect. Woke discourse calls for cultural appreciation grounded in awareness, empathy, and contextual sensitivity, especially in media, fashion, and entertainment.

Politicians, celebrities, and public institutions are increasingly held accountable for their language, symbols, and narratives, particularly when these are perceived as reinforcing exclusion or oppression. Wokeism encourages communicative practices that foster empathy, represent diverse identities accurately, and promote shared understanding across cultural divides.

In essence, wokeism's focus on language and discourse reflects its broader mission: to reshape public norms, disrupt hegemonic narratives, and advance a more inclusive and equitable society.

Gender, Family, and Life Issues

A third central dimension of wokeism addresses shifting conceptions of gender identity, family structures, and life-related ethical concerns. Drawing from the theoretical foundations of Feminist and Queer Theory [16, 17], wokeism fundamentally challenges traditional binaries and normative frameworks by affirming a fluid and expansive understanding of gender. It recognizes a wide range of identities—including nonbinary, transgender, genderqueer, and agender individuals—and promotes legal protections and societal inclusion for those across the LGBTQ+ spectrum.

This inclusive stance has translated into practical reforms, such as the introduction of gender-neutral restrooms in public buildings, the recognition of nonbinary gender markers on official documents in states such as California and Oregon, and antidiscrimination protections in educational institutions and workplaces. Wokeism also fosters safe and affirming spaces by combating hate speech, bullying, and exclusion in schools, universities, and public discourse.

At the heart of this perspective lies a firm commitment to bodily autonomy and the ethical primacy of consent. Whether in romantic, familial, or institutional settings, wokeism insists on the importance of mutual respect, voluntary participation, and the unequivocal rejection of coercion, harassment, and sexual violence. For instance, widespread support for the #MeToo movement illustrates how woke principles advocate for societal accountability in matters of sexual misconduct.

Wokeism further reimagines the concept of family by moving beyond the traditional nuclear model. It affirms a range of familial arrangements, including single-parent households, same-sex parent families, blended families, and chosen families—communities of mutual care not necessarily bound by blood or law. This inclusive understanding has influenced public policy and cultural narratives; for example, countries such as Canada and the Netherlands legally recognize same-sex parenting rights, while TV shows such as *Modern Family* and *Pose* depict nontraditional families with complexity and visibility.

Consistent with Queer Theory [18, 19], wokeism also contests rigid gender roles within domestic life. It encourages shared parenting responsibilities and rejects outdated norms that assign caregiving solely to women. Parental leave policies that are gender-neutral, such as those adopted in Scandinavian countries, exemplify this commitment to domestic equity.

Inclusive family policy is a key priority. This priority includes workplace accommodations for breastfeeding mothers, the establishment of child care support systems, and the adoption of inclusive language in legal, health care, and educational settings that avoids assumptions about family composition. For example, forms that use "parent/guardian" instead of "mother/father" reflect this shift.

Reproductive rights form a cornerstone of woke ideology. Wokeism vigorously defends a woman's right to reproductive autonomy, including access to safe and legal abortion, contraception, and comprehensive reproductive health care. This commitment is reflected in public advocacy and political efforts to protect reproductive rights in jurisdictions such as New York and California, even as access is curtailed elsewhere (Figure 5.2).

In addition to reproductive freedoms, wokeism extends its emphasis on autonomy and dignity to end-of-life issues. It supports the right of terminally ill individuals to make self-determined choices about death, including the right to access euthanasia or physician-assisted dying. Countries such as Canada and Belgium have enacted legislation reflecting this position, emphasizing individual agency in matters of unbearable suffering and terminal illness.

Taken together, these commitments reflect wokeism's broader ethical framework: a deep concern for autonomy, dignity, and the recognition

Gender-Affirming Youth Care Bans in the U.S.

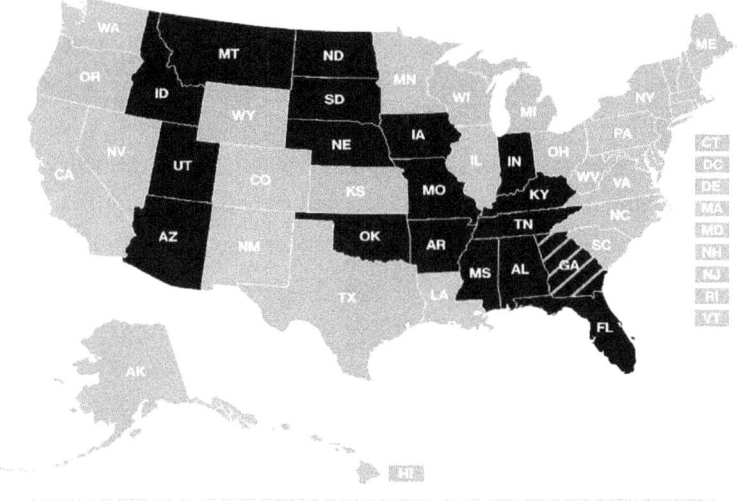

Figure 5.2 Gender affirming care is a controversial issue in the United States

Source: ABC News [20]

of diverse identities and life choices across private and public spheres. Through legal reforms, cultural shifts, and institutional advocacy, wokeism seeks to foster a more inclusive, respectful, and equitable society.

Activism, Allyship, and Media Representation

A fourth dimension of wokeism revolves around activism, allyship, and media representation, reflecting its inherently critical and interventionist nature. Rooted in Critical Theory [21], wokeism promotes active engagement in efforts to dismantle systemic injustice. This movement includes grassroots activism such as protests, public demonstrations, and organized movements that demand political and institutional reform. Notable examples include the *Black Lives Matter* protests, climate justice marches, and advocacy for transgender rights, which mobilize large segments of the population to confront issues of police violence, environmental degradation, and gender-based discrimination.

Wokeism also informs corporate and institutional activism. Many woke-aligned businesses initiate public campaigns to raise awareness about social justice issues, often embedding messages of DEI into their marketing strategies. For instance, Nike's endorsement of Colin Kaepernick—following his protest against police brutality—illustrates how brands use their platform to support progressive causes, even at the risk of public backlash.

A key concept in wokeism is *allyship*, which refers to the active support of marginalized communities by individuals who may not share those identities but are committed to advancing justice and equality. This aspect includes speaking out against racism, sexism, homophobia, or xenophobia in personal and professional contexts. Examples of allyship range from public figures defending LGBTQ+ rights, such as Taylor Swift's advocacy during Pride Month, to individuals amplifying minority voices on social media.

The phenomenon of *cancel culture* also emerges from this context. It involves publicly calling out, criticizing, or boycotting individuals, companies, or institutions that are perceived to have engaged in discriminatory, offensive, or unethical behavior. While supporters see cancel culture as a form of accountability and empowerment for marginalized voices, critics argue that it can become punitive or suppress open dialogue.

Social media plays a crucial role in modern woke activism. Platforms such as Twitter, Instagram, and TikTok are widely used to mobilize support, raise awareness, and coordinate campaigns. Hashtags such as #MeToo, #BlackLivesMatter, and #StopAsianHate have transformed individual grievances into global movements, demonstrating the power of digital platforms to catalyze collective action.

Consistent with Postcolonial Theory and Critical Race Theory [22, 23], wokeism is deeply connected to movements that challenge colonial legacies and racial hierarchies. The Black Lives Matter movement, for example, calls for the eradication of white supremacy and structural violence inflicted upon Black communities by the state and private actors. These efforts reflect wokeism's broader commitment to addressing historical injustices and redistributing social power.

Another essential facet of wokeism involves the critical analysis of media representation. Advocates seek to challenge and transform portrayals that reinforce stereotypes or marginalize minority identities. The critical analysis of media includes pushing for more diverse casting in film and television, nuanced depictions of race, gender, and sexuality, and the dismantling of harmful tropes. For instance, the success of inclusive media projects such as *Pose*, *Black Panther*, or *Bridgerton* reflects a growing demand for narratives that reflect the complexity of diverse experiences.

Finally, wokeism encourages continuous learning and personal development. Advocates emphasize the importance of education, training, and critical self-reflection to remain informed about best practices in equity, diversity, and inclusion. Whether through reading, workshops, or dialogue, individuals are encouraged to interrogate their biases and contribute meaningfully to a more just society.

Woke Environmentalism

The fifth dimension of wokeism centers on environmental justice, underscoring the profound link between ecological concerns and social equity. Drawing upon Critical and Postcolonial Theories [22, 24], wokeism frames environmental degradation not simply as a scientific or technical issue but as a profoundly moral and political one—one that disproportionately affects marginalized and historically oppressed communities.

At the heart of this perspective is the concept of *environmental justice*, which addresses the unequal distribution of environmental harms. Marginalized populations—particularly low-income communities, indigenous peoples, and communities of color—often face greater exposure to air and water pollution, live near hazardous waste sites, and are more vulnerable to the effects of climate change. For instance, residents of Flint, Michigan, suffered a public health crisis when their drinking water was contaminated with lead—an incident widely seen through the lens of racial and environmental injustice.

Wokeism critiques extractive industries such as mining, oil drilling, and deforestation, especially when they encroach on indigenous lands without consent. A prominent example is the opposition to the Dakota Access Pipeline, where indigenous activists and their allies protested against the violation of treaty rights and the environmental risks posed to the Standing Rock Sioux Tribe's water supply. In this context, woke activism calls for the defense of ecosystems, the upholding of indigenous sovereignty, and the rejection of practices rooted in colonial patterns of exploitation.

Moreover, climate change is framed by woke advocates as a global justice issue that magnifies preexisting inequalities. Extreme weather events, food insecurity, and forced migration disproportionately affect the Global South and vulnerable populations in the Global North. Woke environmentalism thus supports climate policies that are not only effective in reducing carbon emissions but also socially equitable—such as green job programs aimed at low-income communities and the divestment from fossil fuels in favor of renewable energy initiatives.

Another key concern is the ethical treatment of animals, which is viewed as part of a broader framework of justice and compassion. Woke perspectives often align with plant-based diets, critiques of factory farming, and animal welfare advocacy as part of an integrated moral response to the exploitation of vulnerable beings—both human and nonhuman.

This environmental consciousness also draws attention to the historical legacy of colonialism in shaping patterns of environmental degradation. From the extraction of natural resources in colonized regions to the forced displacement of indigenous communities, wokeism insists on confronting these legacies in order to build a truly sustainable future. Activists argue that meaningful ecological reform must account for historical injustices and empower those most affected to lead the path forward.

Examples of woke-informed environmental advocacy include the Sunrise Movement in the United States, which pushes for a Green New Deal that merges climate policy with social justice; Greta Thunberg's international school strike campaign, which emphasizes intergenerational equity; and the work of environmental activists like Vandana Shiva, who challenges corporate-driven agriculture in favor of indigenous and local knowledge systems.

In essence, the environmental dimension of wokeism seeks a transformation in both values and policies—moving away from profit-driven exploitation toward models of stewardship, sustainability, and justice. The ultimate goal is to ensure that environmental benefits and protections are equitably distributed and that the voices of those historically excluded from environmental decision making are centered in shaping the future.

Woke Business

The final dimension of wokeism addresses the evolving role of business and capitalism in advancing social justice. Informed by Critical Theory, Postcolonialism, and Intersectionality [22, 23, 25], wokeism offers a critical lens on corporate practices, challenging the traditional emphasis on profit maximization and calling for ethical responsibility across economic systems.

At the core of this perspective is the concept of *corporate accountability*, which demands that businesses consider the social, environmental, and ethical implications of their operations, including reexamining supply chains to avoid forced labor, ensuring fair wages for workers, and fostering ethical relationships with local communities. For example, Patagonia has become a leading example of woke-aligned corporate behavior by committing to environmental sustainability, fair labor practices, and climate activism, including donating a portion of profits to ecological causes.

Wokeism critiques the exploitative dimensions of capitalism, particularly its impact on marginalized populations. It calls out labor exploitation, unsafe working conditions, and the widening gap between executive compensation and worker pay. The backlash against companies like Amazon for warehouse conditions and wage disparities illustrates the growing public demand for equitable labor practices. In response, some companies have adopted wage transparency policies and initiated internal audits to address racial and gender pay gaps.

Environmental sustainability is another primary concern. Woke-oriented businesses are encouraged to reduce their carbon footprint, transition to renewable energy, and commit to green supply chains. For instance, IKEA has invested heavily in solar energy and sustainable forestry to minimize its environmental impact. These measures not only reflect ecological responsibility but also align with consumer expectations in a values-driven marketplace.

Consumer activism plays a key role in this dynamic. Many consumers now make deliberate choices to support brands that align with social justice values—such as Ben & Jerry's outspoken support for racial justice movements—and boycott companies that engage in discriminatory or unethical practices. This shift has given rise to the concept of "voting with your wallet," where spending becomes a form of activism.

Wokeism also calls for a broader reevaluation of capitalism itself. Some advocates argue for systemic economic reforms that would make wealth distribution more equitable and prioritize human well-being over shareholder profits. These discussions are reflected in debates over universal basic income, employee ownership models, and the regulation of monopolistic tech giants.

In the workplace, wokeism emphasizes inclusive corporate cultures and equitable policies, including promoting work–life balance through flexible schedules, remote work options, and comprehensive parental leave policies. Salesforce, for example, offers expansive family leave benefits and conducts regular pay equity audits to close racial and gender wage gaps.

Marketing and representation are equally important. Woke-informed branding avoids harmful stereotypes and aims for authentic representation by featuring individuals from diverse racial, ethnic, gender, and ability backgrounds. Dove's "Real Beauty" campaign, which celebrates body diversity and challenges conventional beauty norms, is a notable example.

Ultimately, wokeism redefines the purpose of business: from maximizing profit to maximizing ethical impact. By urging corporations to engage publicly with social and political issues—such as Nike's stance on racial justice or Unilever's campaigns on gender equality—wokeism envisions businesses as agents of societal transformation. This movement demands a more just, inclusive, and sustainable economic system that places people and the planet above pure profit.

Practical and Managerial Implications of Wokeism

In an increasingly diverse and interconnected global environment, organizations—particularly those in service and knowledge-based sectors—are under growing pressure to integrate woke principles into their strategic planning and operational practices. DEI are no longer viewed merely as moral imperatives but are now recognized as strategic assets that drive innovation, enhance employee engagement, and bolster competitiveness in global markets.

Organizations that thrive in modern economies tend to prioritize inclusive hiring, culturally competent leadership, and the cultivation of workplace environments that foster psychological safety and a sense of belonging. These efforts are not only ethically commendable but also empirically linked to greater creativity, improved decision making, and more agile responses to diverse consumer demands. Concrete DEI strategies may include anonymized recruitment processes to reduce bias, the use of demographic benchmarks to ensure fair representation, and the establishment of diversity councils to oversee implementation and accountability.

Effectively managing a diverse workforce requires a redefined set of leadership competencies. Managers must be trained in inclusive leadership, cultural intelligence, bias awareness, and conflict resolution to navigate the complexities of ideologically and culturally varied teams. Leaders equipped with these skills are better positioned to reduce workplace friction, cultivate collaboration, and foster a respectful and inclusive organizational culture.

As woke values increasingly influence consumer expectations, organizations must ensure that their brand messaging, marketing strategies, and public communications reflect a commitment to social and environmental justice. Ethical branding—when authentic—can significantly enhance public trust and cultivate long-term consumer loyalty. Companies like Ben & Jerry's and Patagonia exemplify this trend by aligning their brand identities with progressive social causes and environmental sustainability.

Wokeism also reshapes the way CSR is understood and enacted. Rather than engaging in symbolic or performative gestures, organizations are expected to take substantive action on pressing social issues, environmental stewardship, and community empowerment. Transparent impact reporting, equity-focused initiatives, and long-term sustainability goals have become integral components of credible CSR. Furthermore, an awareness of cultural trends shaped by wokeism can inform product development and innovation strategies, enabling businesses to design goods and services that resonate with diverse demographics and reflect broader social values.

However, adopting woke principles is not without its challenges. In increasingly polarized political climates, organizations may face backlash or reputational risk for taking strong social positions. To navigate this terrain, companies must develop robust risk management frameworks, including reputation monitoring systems and crisis communication plans. For multinational corporations, the cultural and political reception of DEI initiatives may vary widely across regions, requiring careful adaptation to local norms while maintaining global ethical standards.

Institutionalizing woke values also demands governance models that are transparent, participatory, and inclusive. Organizations may need to revise internal decision-making processes to ensure greater stakeholder engagement, equitable representation, and accountability. Mechanisms such as employee resource groups, stakeholder advisory boards, and participatory policy development can support the effective integration of inclusive governance practices.

Finally, educational institutions play a pivotal role in shaping the next generation of socially conscious leaders. By embedding social justice, ethics, and cultural competency into curricula, schools and universities can prepare students to navigate diverse organizational settings and lead with empathy, equity, and sustainability in mind. Business schools and professional development programs, in particular, must emphasize these values as essential dimensions of responsible and effective leadership.

References

[1] Shastry, V. 2023. *The Merits of "Woke" Capitalism. In The Notorious ESG: Business, Climate, and the Race to Save the Planet*, 81–101. Emerald Publishing Limited.

[2] Fan, J.S. 2019. "Woke Capital: The Role of Corporations in Social Movements." *Harvard Business Law Review* 9, p. 441.

[3] Foss, N.J., and P.G. Klein. 2023. Why do Companies go Woke? *Academy of Management Perspectives* 37, no. 4, pp. 351–367.

[4] Wright, P.M. 2023. "Woke Corporations and Worldview: The Perils of Ceos Making Moral Proclamations from Shaky Moral Foundations." *Academy of Management Perspectives* 37, no. 3, pp. 252–269.

[5] Davies, H.C., and S.E. MacRae. 2023. "Anatomy of the British War on Woke." *Race & Class* 65, no. 2, pp. 3–54.

[6] Weisman, D.L. 2023. "Can You Have Your Corporate Wokeism and Eat it, too?" *The Economists' 20(1), 27–33. Berlin, Germany: De Gruyter.*

[7] Rozado, D. 2023. "The Great Awakening as a Global Phenomenon." arXiv preprint arXiv:2304.01596.

[8] Rozado, D., M. Al-Gharbi, and J. Halberstadt. 2023. "Prevalence of Prejudice-Denoting Words in News Media Discourse: A Chronological Analysis." *Social Science Computer Review* 41, no. 1, pp. 99–122.

[9] Butterworth, B. 2021. What Does 'Woke' Mean? Origins of the term and how the meaning has changed and retrieved September 30, 2021.

[10] McGrath, T. 2019. *Woke: A Guide to Social Justice.* Constable.

[11] Caldera, A. 2018. "Woke Pedagogy: A Framework for Teaching and Learning." *Diversity, Social Justice, and the Educational Leader* 2, no. 3, p. 1.

[12] Jussim, L. 2024. "Diversity is Diverse: Social Justice Reparations and Science." *Perspectives on Psychological Science* 19, no. 3, pp. 564–575.

[13] DiTomaso, N. 2023. "Rethinking "Woke" and "Integrative" Diversity Strategies: Diversity, Equity, Inclusion—and Inequality." *Academy of Management Perspectives* 38, no. 2, amp-2023.

[14] Smith, I.A., A. Griffiths, and K. Harvey. 2023. "Microaggression Terminology in Communications on Twitter: A Corpus Linguistic Analysis." *International Journal of Communication* 17, pp. 2596–2620.

[15] Zavattaro, S.M., and D. Bearfield. 2022. "Weaponization of Wokeness: The Theater of Management and Implications for Public Administration." *Public Administration Review* 82, no. 3, pp. 585–593.

[16] Alcoff, L. 1996. *Feminist Theory and Social Science. Body Space: Destabilizing Geographies of Gender and Sexuality*, 13–27. London: Routledge.

[17] Jagose, A. 2009. "Feminism's Queer Theory." *Feminism & Psychology* 19, no. 2, pp. 157–174.

[18] Pluckrose, H., and J.A. Lindsay. 2020. *Cynical Theories: How Activist Scholarship Made Everything About Race, Gender, and Identity—and Why This Harms Everybody.* US&CA: Pitchstone Publishing.

[19] Watson, K. 2005. "Queer Theory." *Group Analysis* 38, no. 1, pp. 67–81.

[20] ABC News. https://abcnews.go.com/US/map-gender-affirming-care-targeted-us/story?id=97443087

[21] Thompson, M.J., ed. 2017. *The Palgrave Handbook of Critical Theory.* Springer.

[22] Ashcroft, B., G. Griffiths, and H. Tiffin. 2013. *Postcolonial Studies: The Key Concepts.* Routledge.

[23] Delgado, R., and J. Stefancic, J., eds. 2000. *Critical Race Theory: The Cutting Edge.* Temple University Press.

[24] Sandler, R. D., and P.C. Pezzullo., eds. 2007. *Environmental Justice and Environmentalism: The Social Justice Challenge to the Environmental Movement.* MIT Press.

[25] Cho, S., K.W. Crenshaw, and L. McCall. 2013. "Toward a Field of Intersectionality Studies: Theory, Applications, and Praxis." *Signs: Journal of Women in Culture and Society* 38, no. 4, 785–810.

CHAPTER 6

The Changing Landscape of Global Affairs

The Rise of a Multipolar World Order

Since the end of the Cold War, the global system has undergone a profound transformation, marked by the emergence of a multipolar world governed by multiple centers of political and economic decision making [1]. The collapse of the Soviet Union and the decline of communist regimes in the early 1990s ended the era of global bipolarity that had defined international relations since World War II. During the Cold War, power was concentrated in the hands of two superpowers—the United States and the Soviet Union. However, over the past two decades, a more decentralized and polycentric global structure has emerged. States such as China, India, Brazil, Russia, Japan, and members of the EU have become increasingly prominent players in international politics and economics [1, 2].

This evolving multipolarity is not only driven by the redistribution of power among states but also by the growing significance of nonstate actors, including MNCs, sovereign wealth funds, financial markets, technology firms, and supranational and regional institutions. As power becomes more fragmented, global governance has become more complex, marked by overlapping spheres of influence and increasing interdependence [3]. In parallel with these political changes, the global economy has also entered a multipolar phase [4].

Globalization has enabled a group of emerging economies to achieve remarkable growth, despite not being fully industrialized or socially advanced [5]. Between 2005 and 2010, for instance, economies such as China and India grew at over 6 percent per year, far surpassing the sub-2 percent growth of most advanced Western nations [4]. These trends have had tangible developmental consequences. In China, gross national income (GNI) per capita increased more than sevenfold between 1990 and 2008, and the percentage of the population living on less than $1.25 a day fell from nearly 60 to 16 percent over the same period [4]. Likewise, countries such as Brazil, India, and South Africa have experienced significant improvements in infrastructure, poverty alleviation, and technology adoption.

The rise of emerging markets is also evident in global trade and investment flows. The share of global exports originating from developing countries increased from 28 percent in 1990 to 42 percent in 2007. Similarly, the proportion of FDI going to these countries rose from 18 percent to 33 percent between 1990 and 2006 [5]. FDI inflows to developing economies surged from $12 billion in 1990 to nearly $328 billion by 2010, representing 24.8 percent of global FDI [6]. Meanwhile, the shares of global FDI attributed to traditional powers such as the United States and Japan have declined, underscoring the growing role of emerging countries in the international financial landscape [7, 8]. Today, developing nations generate more than half of global GDP, dominate global energy consumption, and account for a growing number of Fortune Global 500 corporations [9–11].

Nevertheless, these economies continue to face significant challenges in governance, regulatory efficiency, and education compared to advanced industrialized nations [12]. According to the MSCI Emerging Markets Index (2020), 21 countries—including Brazil, China, India, Indonesia, Mexico, South Africa, and Turkey—are classified as emerging markets (http://msci.com). Goldman Sachs projects that by 2040, the BRIC nations—Brazil, Russia, India, and China—will collectively surpass the economic output of the G7 countries (the United States, Japan, Germany, France, the United Kingdom, Italy, and Canada) [13]. Furthermore, an expanded group of emerging economies—including Bangladesh, Egypt, Indonesia, Iran, South Korea, Mexico, Nigeria, Pakistan, the Philippines, Turkey, and Vietnam—is expected to outpace the G7 shortly after 2030.

As their economic weight increases, these countries are asserting themselves more forcefully on the global stage. Institutions established after World War II—such as the IMF and the World Bank—have come under pressure to adapt their governance structures better to reflect the new distribution of power [14]. The shift from the G8 to the G20 in 2008 symbolizes this transition. Similar reforms have been pursued at the IMF, and debates continue regarding the expansion and restructuring of the United Nations Security Council [5].

The most recent BRICS Summit in Rio de Janeiro marked a critical step in institutionalizing multipolarity. With the admission of Indonesia and growing cooperation with Egypt, Ethiopia, Iran, and the UAE, the BRICS+ coalition now accounts for over 45 percent of global GDP and more than half of the world's population. The Rio Declaration emphasized state sovereignty, AI governance, South–South cooperation, and institutional reform—challenging the dominance of Western-led institutions such as the UN and WTO.

Western powers, particularly the United States, have responded with ambivalence. In 2025, Washington imposed tariffs on several BRICS countries, prompting calls from Brazil's leadership for a coordinated response through the G20. India, meanwhile, continues to pursue strategic autonomy—engaging with BRICS while deepening its ties with ASEAN and Indo-Pacific nations. This dual-track diplomacy reflects a broader desire among emerging powers to shape global norms without succumbing to the dominance of any single state or bloc.

As Fareed Zakaria (2011) argued, the world is experiencing the third major power shift in modern history. The first occurred in the 15th century with the rise of the Western world and the transformation of science, commerce, and politics. The second shift, in the late 19th century, brought the United States to global preeminence. The third shift—currently underway—is characterized by what Zakaria calls "the rise of the rest." While the United States remains dominant in military terms, its superiority in industrial, financial, technological, and cultural spheres is increasingly being contested [1, 14]. For the first time since the Industrial Revolution, the global economy is no longer controlled by a handful of Western nations. The ascent of emerging powers represents a historic inflection point—arguably the most significant structural transformation in the international system since the 18th century [13, 15] (Figure 6.1).

Figure 6.1 Emerging economies have consistently outperformed advanced economies in the past 20 years

Source: IMF [21]

What Decline? Do Not Bet Against America, Yet!

The notion of "the rise of the rest" suggests a fundamental shift in global power, with the implication that the United States is undergoing significant economic and geopolitical decline. This view posits that other countries are poised to capitalize on American weakness and challenge its position as the world's preeminent power. It is a narrative that has gained traction not only among ordinary citizens but also among media commentators and political analysts who have long anticipated America's imminent fall from global leadership [16].

Proponents of this view, often labeled "declinists," interpret the rise of emerging economies as a harbinger of doom for the United States. They fear that globalization, technological shifts, and demographic trends will undermine America's foreign policy capabilities and jeopardize global stability [17]. In support of their argument, declinists frequently cite domestic issues within the United States—such as a faltering education system, a shrinking middle class, and political gridlock—as indicators of inevitable decline [18]. However, this narrative is neither new nor remarkably accurate. Since the 1960s, commentators have regularly predicted America's decline, each time forecasting a decisive turning point that never fully materialized [19, 20].

The assumption that China or other emerging powers are poised to eclipse the United States is often based on an exaggerated reading of global trends. The reality is more nuanced. The United States remains the world's largest economy and is likely to retain this position for the foreseeable future. Despite the rise of countries such as China and India, the U.S. share of global GDP has remained relatively stable over the past three decades [4]. As of 2024, the United States—home to less than 4.2 percent of the world's population—accounts for approximately 26.3 percent of global nominal GDP, maintaining its position as the world's largest economy. In contrast, China, which comprises about 17.8 percent of the global population, contributes roughly 16.8 percent of global GDP [21]. Thus, while China has narrowed the gap, the U.S. economy remains significantly larger relative to its population size, underscoring its continued economic dominance and productivity advantage.

The strength of the American economy remains striking when examined at both national and subnational levels. California, the largest U.S. state economy, now boasts a GDP exceeding $4.3 trillion, making it the fifth-largest economy in the world, ahead of India, Russia, and Brazil individually [21]. Texas, with a GDP of over $2.4 trillion, rivals the entire economic output of countries such as South Korea and Canada, and still surpasses Russia in nominal terms. At the national level, the U.S. economy, valued at approximately $27.7 trillion, remains larger than the combined economies of China, Japan, Germany, and the United Kingdom, whose cumulative GDP falls short of the U.S. total [22].

In terms of standard of living, the disparities remain substantial. According to World Bank data, U.S. GDP per capita is approximately $83,000, compared to $14,000 in Brazil, $13,000 in China, and just over $2,700 in India—making the American standard of living roughly 6 times higher than China's, nearly 6 times higher than Brazil's, and more than 30 times higher than India's [21]. These figures reinforce the persistent economic dominance of the United States, not just in size but also in terms of productivity and quality of life.

Beyond economic size, the United States enjoys unparalleled structural advantages—spanning geography, natural resources, climate, and access to energy. One of its most enduring strengths lies in its control over the global financial architecture, particularly through the U.S. dollar's role as the dominant reserve currency. As former French President Charles de Gaulle observed, this position provides the United States with an "exorbitant privilege." By anchoring the international monetary system to the dollar, the United States effectively benefits from what is akin to a global tax, allowing it to receive more than it contributes to the provision of international public goods [23].

Another critical element of U.S. resilience is its global competitiveness. While China, India, and Brazil are often cited as rising giants, they lag in terms of economic efficiency and innovation. According to the World Economic Forum, the United States has consistently ranked among the world's most competitive economies, whereas the BRICS countries frequently occupy lower tiers [24]. Innovation, in particular, remains a cornerstone of American strength. As of 2008, the United States accounted for 40 percent of total global spending on R&D. Moreover, two-thirds of the most highly cited researchers in science and technology were based in the United States [24]. Even as global investment in R&D has expanded, the United States remains a leader in technological innovation and patent production.

This advantage extends to the corporate sector. In 2020, 22 of the world's top 50 corporations were American [25]. In contrast, many firms in emerging economies remain uncompetitive, heavily reliant on government support, and often lacking in managerial acumen and international brand presence. For example, a substantial portion of China's major enterprises are state-owned, domestically focused, and plagued by issues related to transparency and strategic coherence [26].

Perhaps the most decisive marker of American global primacy is its military capability. The United States continues to outspend all other nations on defense, allocating $778 billion to its military in 2020—accounting for 39 percent of total global defense spending [27]. Although China has increased its defense budget steadily since 1989, its military expenditure remains less than one-fifth that of the United States. In addition to its unmatched hardware and strategic reach, the United States also commands the world's most extensive and enduring network of global alliances.

In soft power, the United States also remains unrivaled. Its pluralistic political culture and open educational system continue to attract international talent from across the globe, including from countries such as China and Russia that are often critical of American foreign policy. American universities are widely regarded as world leaders; in 2020, 8 of the top 10 global universities were located in the United States [28, 29]. These institutions not only elevate professional credentials but also impart essential critical thinking and analytical skills. By contrast, educational systems in emerging countries such as Brazil, Russia, China, and India face major structural hurdles that impede their global competitiveness [30].

Taken together, the evidence strongly suggests that American decline is far from inevitable. While the world is undoubtedly becoming more multipolar, the United States continues to possess an extraordinary set of advantages—economic, strategic, technological, and cultural—that ensure its enduring preeminence on the global stage. As history has repeatedly demonstrated, betting against America has rarely been a winning strategy.

The European Union: An Economic Giant and a Political Dwarf

With 27 member states, a population of approximately 450 million, a GDP exceeding $19 trillion in 2024, and consistently high standards of living, the EU remains one of the largest and most influential economic and political entities in the world. The EU's rich cultural legacy, extensive global trade networks, and long-standing traditions in diplomacy and governance secure its place as a major actor in the international system. Developed through centuries of industrialization, colonization, and interstate cooperation, Europe helped shape the architecture of modern international relations. Many of today's global institutions—including the United Nations, IMF, and World Bank—were largely influenced or established by Western European powers such as Britain, France, and Germany. As a result, the EU, alongside the United States, continues to exert considerable influence over the creation, interpretation, and enforcement of international norms across domains such as trade, finance, security, science, education, and human rights. For instance, France remains a permanent member of the UN Security Council, and several other EU countries routinely serve as rotating members [31].

Since the early 2000s, and especially following the publication of the 2003 European Security Strategy, the EU has expressed its intent to take on broader responsibilities in international affairs. It has sought to present itself as a "civilian power"—a champion of peace, multilateralism, development, and human rights. This positioning is evident in its engagement with the Iran nuclear deal (JCPOA), the Paris Climate Accord, and development programs in Africa and Southeast Asia. In contrast to the more unilateral or hard-power-oriented approaches of the United States or China, the EU often prefers negotiation, consensus-building, and multilateral diplomacy [32].

As a result, in many regions of the world—particularly in Africa, Latin America, and parts of Asia—the EU enjoys a relatively high degree of trust, seen as a stable and cooperative partner rather than a hegemonic power. This trust provides the EU with considerable soft power, rooted in its normative appeal rather than coercive capacity. However, this reliance on diplomatic influence also reveals its limitations: the EU has often failed to exert significant influence on global crises where military or coercive tools are essential.

Indeed, the EU's lack of a unified defense and security policy remains one of its most persistent weaknesses. While countries like France have strong national militaries and nuclear capabilities, the EU as a whole lacks a centralized military command or rapid-response force capable of projecting power or ensuring the collective security of the bloc. The European Defense Fund (EDF) and initiatives such as Permanent Structured Cooperation (PESCO) have made some progress in recent years. However, they fall short of what is needed for genuine strategic autonomy.

Moreover, the EU still struggles to implement a cohesive and independent foreign policy. The war in Ukraine, now in its third year as of 2024, has both galvanized and tested EU unity. While the EU has imposed sanctions on Russia, provided humanitarian and military support to Ukraine, and accelerated efforts to reduce dependence on Russian energy, internal divisions remain. Hungary, for instance, has repeatedly slowed down or vetoed collective action, illustrating the enduring challenges of consensus-based decision-making within the bloc.

Economic uncertainty also persists. Although the eurozone avoided a major crisis in 2023, inflation, energy instability following the war in Ukraine, and divergent fiscal policies among member states have raised questions about the long-term sustainability of the euro. The EU Green Deal, while ambitious, has faced pushback from both member states and sectors fearing economic dislocation. These issues have affected not only global perceptions of the EU model but also domestic confidence in European integration [31].

The European Council on Foreign Relations has noted that Europe appears to be losing its strategic agency. Where it was once seen as part of the solution to international problems, it is now increasingly perceived as a passive or reactive actor [33]. In many geopolitical arenas—such as the Indo-Pacific, the Sahel, or the Middle East—the EU has limited capacity to shape events, and often follows the lead of either the United States or dominant regional powers.

The EU's overrepresentation in global institutions is also under increasing scrutiny. As emerging powers such as India, Brazil, Indonesia, and Nigeria grow in economic and political weight, there are growing calls for a more equitable distribution of influence in institutions such as the UN Security Council, IMF, and World Bank. The enduring dominance of European nations in these forums is increasingly challenged by countries advocating for global governance reform that reflects current demographic and economic realities [31].

In light of these developments, the EU continues to face a strategic crossroads. If it succeeds in deepening political integration, creating a credible collective security apparatus, and speaking with a united voice on major international issues, it could enhance its global influence significantly. However, if internal divisions persist and the EU fails to adapt to shifting global power dynamics, it risks declining relevance as newer powers shape the contours of the 21st-century order.

Despite its economic might, the EU's global influence remains constrained by institutional complexity, political fragmentation, and limited military capacity. This reality continues to justify the long-standing characterization of the EU as an "economic giant and a political dwarf" [32].

The Rise of Nonstate Actors

The Treaty of Westphalia of 1648 laid the foundation for the modern international system by enshrining the principle of state sovereignty. This principle held that each nation-state possessed authority over its own territory and internal affairs, free from external interference. For centuries, this Westphalian model remained central to global order. However, by the late 20th century—especially following the end of the Cold War—this model began to erode under the combined pressures of globalization, digital transformation, transnational interdependence, and the growing influence of nonstate actors.

In today's international landscape, nonstate actors have emerged as increasingly important forces, often rivaling or even surpassing states in specific domains of influence. These actors are nonsovereign entities that exercise significant economic, political, or social power on the national and international stages [34]. They encompass a broad array of organizations and networks: international organizations (e.g., the United Nations, World Health Organization [WHO]), MNCs, nongovernmental organizations (NGOs), scientific and expert communities, private military contractors, transnational criminal and terrorist networks, and global advocacy coalitions [35–38].

One of the most profound consequences of this shift has been the fragmentation of global governance [39]. While states continue to serve as the principal actors in formal diplomacy, they increasingly share the stage with agile and influential nonstate actors. This feature has led to both cooperation and competition between state and nonstate forces across a wide range of global issues—from climate change and cybersecurity to humanitarian relief and financial regulation.

The economic rise of MNCs is among the most visible indicators of nonstate influence. These companies, with global supply chains, vast data assets, and resources that rival many countries' GDPs, often shape international economic policy. In 2023, Apple's market capitalization exceeded $3 trillion, making it more valuable than the GDP of over 150 countries. As of 2024, Amazon, Alphabet, and Saudi Aramco similarly operate with budgets and capabilities that allow them to influence not only global markets but also national policies on taxation, labor standards, data privacy, and sustainability.

The number of MNCs has exploded from just 7,000 in 1972 to more than 80,000 active firms today, with hundreds of thousands of affiliates around the world [40]. Their influence is also felt in international climate negotiations, where companies such as Tesla, Unilever, and

Microsoft have made climate pledges that surpass the commitments of many nation-states.

NGOs have similarly become indispensable players in international relations. Often more flexible and responsive than national governments, NGOs operate across borders to address issues such as poverty, education, climate change, and human rights. As of 2024, over 5,000 NGOs hold consultative status with the United Nations Economic and Social Council (ECOSOC), reflecting their growing role in global governance [40].

Organizations such as Médecins Sans Frontières, Greenpeace, and the International Crisis Group influence policy decisions, shape public opinion, and in some cases, implement services that states either neglect or are incapable of delivering. In crisis regions, NGOs have often substituted for state functions in providing health care, education, and humanitarian assistance.

Another notable dimension of nonstate influence is the rise of ultrawealthy individuals—tech moguls, media tycoons, philanthropists, and activist celebrities—who leverage their wealth and platforms to shape global discourse and public policy. Entrepreneurs like Elon Musk, Jeff Bezos, and Bill Gates not only influence technological innovation but also engage in space exploration, vaccine development, and climate initiatives. The Bill & Melinda Gates Foundation, for example, has invested billions in global health and development and plays a central role in international public health decision making—often with more agility than multilateral institutions [41].

Meanwhile, influential activists such as Greta Thunberg have galvanized global climate movements, reshaping the narrative around environmental responsibility, especially among younger generations.

Not all nonstate actors serve constructive roles. The past two decades have witnessed the rise of transnational criminal organizations, drug cartels, and terrorist networks that operate across weak borders and challenge national authorities. These include well-organized groups such as the Sinaloa Cartel, ISIS-affiliated cells, and cybercriminal syndicates such as REvil and Lazarus Group, who conduct ransomware attacks, espionage, and digital extortion.

Some violent nonstate actors, such as Hezbollah in Lebanon, the Taliban in Afghanistan, and the Wagner Group in Africa, have come to wield influence rivaling or even exceeding that of the central government. These organizations often provide social services, enforce local governance, or manage natural resources in fragile states. In some cases, they benefit from external state sponsorship, blurring the boundaries between public and private force [42].

What emerges today is not a zero-sum battle between states and nonstate actors, but a hybrid governance system in which roles are increasingly shared, overlapping, or contested. States continue to wield legal authority, but nonstate actors increasingly fill functional, normative, and operational gaps in global governance. In areas such as climate change, pandemic response, AI regulation, and humanitarian intervention, multistakeholder models that involve businesses, NGOs, and epistemic communities are becoming the norm.

The rise of nonstate actors reflects a fundamental transformation in the architecture of global power. While the Westphalian notion of state sovereignty remains formally intact, the realpolitik of international relations is increasingly shaped by a polycentric network of actors whose legitimacy derives not from territorial control but from their resources, expertise, reach, and agility. The challenge ahead will be managing this complex ecosystem of global influence in a way that maintains accountability, enhances cooperation, and fosters inclusive governance in a multipolar world.

The Comeback of Interstate Military Conflicts and Nuclear Arsenals

The early 21st century has witnessed a resurgence of traditional geopolitical tensions that many believed had been relegated to history. Two particularly concerning trends have emerged: the return of interstate military conflicts and the increasing salience of nuclear weapons. These developments signify a shift away from post-Cold War optimism and reflect a deteriorating global security environment shaped by the erosion of multilateral institutions, renewed great power rivalries, and the breakdown of arms control regimes.

For much of the post-1990s era, asymmetric threats posed by nonstate actors dominated the global security agenda. However, the landscape has shifted dramatically as traditional interstate conflicts have reemerged with force.

The most significant and ongoing example is Russia's full-scale invasion of Ukraine in February 2022. This conflict marked the largest interstate war in Europe since World War II, involving annexations of Ukrainian territories, massive deployments of conventional forces, and frequent use of long-range missile and drone attacks. The conflict has revitalized NATO, triggered increased defense expenditures across Europe, and signaled a return to Cold War-era security dynamics.

Beyond Europe, East Asia has become another focal point of military friction. China's increasingly assertive behavior in the South China Sea and around Taiwan has heightened fears of future conflict. Regular incursions into Taiwan's airspace and large-scale military drills reinforce the potential for escalation. Additionally, the 2020 border clashes between India and China in Ladakh demonstrated that even nuclear-armed states are willing to engage in direct military confrontations.

North Korea further complicates the regional security landscape. Its persistent ballistic missile tests and nuclear brinkmanship have not only destabilized Northeast Asia but also prompted a trilateral security response from the United States, Japan, and South Korea, with discussions intensifying around nuclear sharing and defensive posturing.

The Middle East also continues to experience escalating interstate tensions. The 2023–2024 Israel–Hamas war intensified concerns about a broader regional conflict, especially given the overlapping proxy dynamics involving Iran and Hezbollah. The ongoing shadow conflict between Israel and Iran, characterized by cyber warfare, assassinations, and drone strikes, exemplifies how hybrid forms of interstate conflict have become normalized. Similarly, the Yemen conflict has expanded from a civil war into a multinational confrontation involving Saudi Arabia, the UAE, and Iran.

Meanwhile, global defense postures are shifting from counterterrorism to high-intensity conflict preparedness. Strategic doctrines in the United States, China, Russia, and NATO increasingly prioritize near-peer competition, emphasizing the acquisition of hypersonic weapons, the militarization of space, enhanced cyber capabilities, and record-breaking defense budgets.

The weakening of international institutions exacerbates these trends. The paralysis of the United Nations Security Council, the collapse of the Intermediate-Range Nuclear Forces (INF) Treaty, and the withdrawal from the Open Skies Treaty have significantly reduced global capacity to prevent and manage interstate conflicts. In the absence of strong multilateral mechanisms, states are increasingly inclined to act unilaterally or preemptively.

The Comeback of Nuclear Arsenals: Strategic Instability in the 21st Century

A troubling resurgence in nuclear weapons policy accompanies this return to interstate rivalry. As of 2024, an estimated 12,500 nuclear warheads are possessed by nine states: Russia (5,580), the United States (5,244), China (500+), France (290), the United Kingdom (225), Pakistan (170), India (164), Israel (90), and North Korea (30–40) (Federation of American Scientists, 2024). While this total is lower than Cold War peaks, it marks a halt in disarmament and a renewed focus on nuclear modernization.

The United States has initiated an extensive modernization of its nuclear triad, including the Sentinel ICBMs, Columbia-class submarines, and B-21 bombers. The 2022 Nuclear Posture Review maintained a policy of deterrence but underscored the need for credible strategic capabilities amid rising threats.

Russia, with the world's largest arsenal, continues to see nuclear weapons as a central element of its defense policy. In 2023, it suspended participation in the New START treaty, the last major arms control agreement with the United States, and has deployed tactical nuclear weapons to Belarus. Its forward-deployed nuclear-capable systems in Kaliningrad highlight a strategy of integrating nuclear threats into conventional military operations, especially in the context of the war in Ukraine.

In Asia, nuclear competition is intensifying. China is rapidly developing a complete nuclear triad, expanding its arsenal beyond 500 warheads, constructing missile silos, and investing in submarine-launched ballistic missiles and hypersonic vehicles. These efforts reflect a strategic calculus shaped by U.S. military presence in the Indo-Pacific and India's growing capabilities.

India maintains a policy of credible minimum deterrence but is investing in multiple independently targetable reentry vehicle (MIRV) technology and sea-based deterrents to counter both China and Pakistan. Pakistan, which follows a first-use doctrine, continues to expand its tactical nuclear weapons program and is one of the fastest-growing nuclear powers globally. Political instability and the risk of extremist infiltration further exacerbate global concerns about nuclear security in the region.

In the Middle East, Israel maintains nuclear ambiguity outside the Nonproliferation Treaty (NPT) framework. It views its nuclear arsenal as vital for national survival in a volatile region and has repeatedly targeted Iran's nuclear infrastructure. Since the U.S. withdrawal from the JCPOA, Iran has accelerated its enrichment activities, bringing it closer to weapons-grade levels, as confirmed by the IAEA's 2024 report.

North Korea has meanwhile demonstrated significant technological progress, including solid-fuel ICBMs and miniaturized tactical nuclear warheads. Its nuclear strategy appears aimed not only at deterrence but also at coercion. These developments have reignited debates in South Korea and Japan about acquiring independent deterrent capabilities or participating in nuclear sharing.

The arms control architecture that helped mitigate nuclear risks in the 20th century is now fragmenting. With the collapse of the INF and Open Skies treaties and the uncertain future of the New START agreement, strategic stability is increasingly tenuous. China refuses to participate in arms control talks, arguing that its arsenal remains limited compared to those of the United States and Russia. Moreover, although over 90 countries have ratified the Treaty on the Prohibition of Nuclear Weapons (TPNW), it is disregarded by all nuclear-armed states.

References

[1] Zakaria, F. 2011. *The Post-American World: Release 2.0 (International Edition)*. New York, NY: W.W. Norton and Company.

[2] Schweller, R.L., and X. Pu. 2011. "After Unipolarity: China's Visions of International Order in an Era of US Decline." *International Security* 36, no. 1, pp. 41–72.

[3] Chan, G. 2013. "The Rise of Multipolarity, the Reshaping of Order: China in a Brave New World?+." *International Journal of China Studies* 4, no. 1, p. 1.

[4] Zoellick, R. 2010. *The End of the Third World?* Washington, DC: Address Delivered Before the Woodrow Wilson Center for International Scholars.

[5] Berliner, J. 2010. The Rise of the Rest: How New Economic Powers are Reshaping the Globe, The Second in a Series of White Papers on the American Economy in a New Era of Globalization. NDN.com

[6] Dohse, D., R. Hassink, and C. Klaerding. 2012. "Emerging Multinationals, International Knowledge Flows and Economic Geography: A Research Agenda." Kiel Working Paper, No.1776.

[7] Kothari, T., M. Kotabe, and P. Murphy. 2013. "Rules of the Game for Emerging Market Multinational Companies from China and India." *Journal of International Management* 19, no. 3, pp. 276–99.

[8] Ramamurti, R. 2012. "Competing with Emerging Market Multinationals." *Business Horizons* 55, no. 3, pp. 241–49.

[9] Kumaraswamy, A., R. Mudambi, H. Saranga, and A. Tripathy. 2012. "Catch-Up Strategies in the Indian Auto Components Industry: Domestic Firms' Responses to Market Liberalization." *Journal of International Business Studies* 43, no. 4, pp. 368–95.

[10] Lorenzen, M., and R. Mudambi. 2012. "Clusters, Connectivity, and CatchUp: Bollywood and Bangalore in the Global Economy." *Journal of Economic Geography* 13, no. 3, pp. 501–34.

[11] Moghaddam, K., D. Sethi, T. Weber, and J. Wu. 2014. "The Smirk of Emerging Market Firms: A Modification of Dunning's Typology of Internationalization Motivations." *Journal of International Management* 20, pp. 359–74.

[12] Banalieva, E.R., L. Tihanyi, T.M. Devinney, and T. Pedersen. 2015. "Introduction to Part II: Emerging Economies and Multinational Enterprises." In *Emerging Economies and Multinational Enterprises (Advances in International Management)*, 43–69. 28 vols. Emerald Group Publishing Limited.

[13] Van Agtmael, A. 2007. "The Emerging Markets Century: How a New Breed of World-Class Companies is Overtaking the World." Available at SimonandSchuster.com

[14] Birdsall, N., and F. Fukuyama. 2011. "The Post-Washington Consensus-Development After the Crisis." *Foreign Affairs* 90, p. 45.

[15] Yeganeh, K.H. 2016. "An Examination of the Conditions, Characteristics, and Strategies About the Rise of Emerging Markets Multinationals." *European Business Review* 28, no. 5, pp. 600–26.

[16] Layne, C. 2012. "This Time It is Real: The End of Unipolarity and the Pax Americana." *International Studies Quarterly* 56, no. 1, pp. 203–13.

[17] Quinn, A. 2011. "The Art of Declining Politely: Obama's Prudent Presidency and the Waning of American Power." *International Affairs* 87, no. 4, pp. 803–24.

[18] Luce, E. 2012. *Time to Start Linking: America in the Age of Descent.* New York: Atlantic Monthly Press.

[19] Calleo, D.P. 2009. *Follies of Power: America's Unipolar Fantasy.* Cambridge University Press.

[20] Wade, R. 2013. "The Art of Power Maintenance: How Western States Keep the Lead in Global Organizations." *Challenge* 56, no. 1, pp. 5–39.

[21] IMF. International Monetary Fund, World Economic Outlook 2024. https://www.imf.org/en/Publications/WEO

[22] International Monetary Fund. https://www.imf.org/external/pubs/ft/ar/2024/

[23] Norrlof, C. 2010. *America's Global Advantage: US Hegemony and International Cooperation.* Cambridge University Press.

[24] Galama, T., and Hosek, J. 2008. *US Competitiveness in Science and Technology.* Santa Monica, CA: Rand Corporation.

[25] The Forbes Magazine List. https://www.forbes.com/just-companies/#473da3f62bf0

[26] Shambaugh, D. 2012. "Are China's Multinational Corporations Really Multinational?" *East Asia Forum Quarterly* 4, no. 2, pp. 7–14.

[27] da Silva, D.L., N. Tian, and A. Marksteiner. 2021. *Trends in World Military Expenditure, 2020.* SIPRI.

[28] QS World University Rankings. 2012. https://topuniversities.Com/university-rankings/world-university-rankings/2012

[29] https://www.forbes.com/sites/nickmorrison/2020/09/02/oxford-keeps-top-spot-but-china-is-the-real-winner-as-us-declines/?sh=6a81e8c742a7

[30] Luce, E. 2012. *Time to Start Linking: America in the Age of Descent.* Grove/Atlantic, Inc.

[31] Smith, K.E. 2013. "Can the European Union be a Pole in a Multipolar World?" *The International Spectator* 48, no. 2, pp. 114–26.

[32] Messner, D. 2007. The European Union: Protagonist in a Multilateral World Order or Peripheral Power in the "Asia-Pacific" Century?.

[33] European Council on Foreign Relations. 2012. "Introduction." *European Foreign Policy Scorecard* 9. http://ecfr.eu/content/entry/european_foreign_policy_scorecard_2012

[34] La-Porte, M.T. 2015. The Legitimacy and Effectiveness of Nonstate Actors and the Public Diplomacy Concept.

[35] Moravcsik, A. 2010. "Europe, the Second Superpower." *Current History* 109, no. 725, p. 91.

[36] Dingwerth, K., and P. Pattberg. 2006. "Global Governance as a Perspective on World Politics." *Global Governance: A Review of Multilateralism and International Organizations* 12, no. 2, pp. 185–203.

[37] Biermann, F., and P.H. Pattberg, eds. 2012. *Global Environmental Governance Reconsidered.* MIT Press.

[38] Karns, M.P., and K.A. Mingst. 2013. "International Organizations and Diplomacy." *In the Oxford Handbook of Modern Diplomacy*. UK: Oxford Academic.

[39] Jang, J., J. McSparren, and Y. Rashchupkina. 2016. "Global Governance: Present and Future." *Palgrave Communications* 2, no. 1, p. 15045.

[40] Falkner, R. 2011. *Global Governance: The Rise of Nonstate Actors: A Background Report for the SOER 2010 Assessment of Global Megatrends*. European Environment Agency.

[41] Bieler, A., R. Higgott, and G. Underhill, eds. 2004. *Nonstate Actors and Authority in the Global System*. Routledge.

[42] Jakobi, A.P 2010. Nonstate Violence and Political Order: A View on Long-Term Consequences of Nonstate Security Governance.

CHAPTER 7

The Inequality, the Wealth Concentration, and the Superrich

The Rise of Economic Inequality in America

For much of the 20th century, economic inequality in the United States remained relatively stable, even declining during certain decades. The post-World War II period, especially between 1947 and the early 1970s, saw real incomes rise across all income groups, with low- and middle-income earners making substantial gains. Strong labor unions, robust collective bargaining, progressive taxation, and a political commitment to full employment and equitable growth underpinned this trend [1, 2]. During these decades, productivity growth translated directly into wage growth, ensuring that the benefits of economic expansion were broadly shared [2].

This balance began to erode in the late 1970s and accelerated through the 1980s (Figures 7.1 and 7.2). Structural economic changes, deregulation, globalization, the weakening of unions, and tax reforms that disproportionately favored the wealthy shifted the distribution of income [4]. By 2023, inequality had reached levels not seen since the Gilded Age. The share of national income held by the top 1 percent rose from about 8 percent in 1979 to over 20 percent in 2021; when capital gains are included, this figure approached 25 percent [5, 6]. Much of this growth came from investment income and capital gains.

While worker productivity continued to climb, real compensation for most Americans stagnated. Between 2000 and 2008, productivity rose sharply, but real wages for the bottom 80 percent of earners remained flat or declined [7]. Since 1990, incomes for the top 1 percent have increased

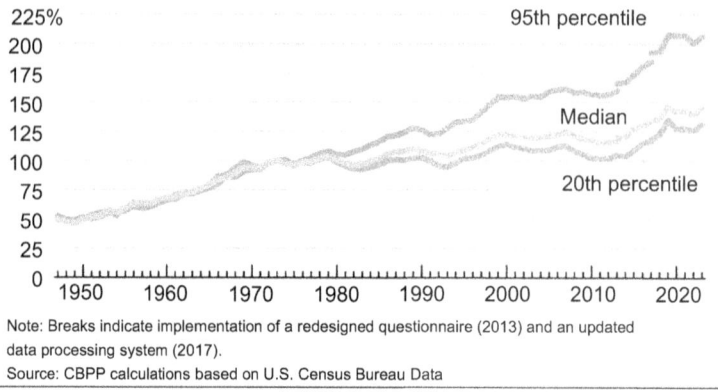

Note: Breaks indicate implementation of a redesigned questionnaire (2013) and an updated data processing system (2017).

Source: CBPP calculations based on U.S. Census Bureau Data

CENTER ON BUDGET AND POLICY PRIORITIES | CBPP.ORG

Figure 7.1 *Real family income 1947–2023, as a percentage of the 1973 level*

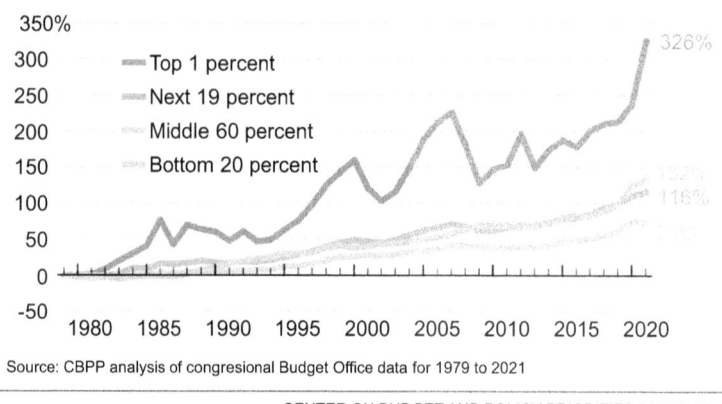

Source: CBPP analysis of congresional Budget Office data for 1979 to 2021

CENTER ON BUDGET AND POLICY PRIORITIES | CBPP.ORG

Figure 7.2 *Percentage change in income after transfers and taxes since 1979*

by nearly 300 percent, while those for the bottom half of the population have barely moved [8]. Today, the top 1 percent of Americans own roughly one-third of all wealth. The nation's billionaire class—more than 700 individuals—controls over $4.5 trillion in assets [45]. Meanwhile, median household income has remained largely stagnant since the early 2000s after adjusting for inflation.

Globally, the United States ranks among the most unequal advanced economies, surpassed in income inequality by only a few developing nations. Unlike other wealthy countries, its tax-and-transfer system does comparatively little to mitigate inequality. The top marginal income tax rate, once 70 percent in 1980, had fallen to 37 percent by 2023 [9], and capital gains are often taxed at lower rates than wages. Efforts to implement wealth taxes have faced strong political resistance. Intergenerational wealth transfer—through inheritance and trusts—further entrenches inequality, reducing social mobility. The income gap between high-earning professionals, executives, and business owners on one hand, and white- and blue-collar workers on the other, has widened sharply over the past four decades [10]. While the U.S. economy continues to grow, the distribution of its gains has become increasingly skewed, creating a new era of stratification in which the fortunes of the wealthy are increasingly detached from the economic realities of the majority.

Economic inequality in the United States is evident in everyday life—shaping cities, neighborhoods, schools, health care systems, and social opportunities. Socioeconomic segregation has intensified, influencing access to resources and long-term life prospects.

One key indicator is the fragility of retirement security. Nearly half of U.S. retirees are expected to outlive their savings, forcing many to work beyond traditional retirement age [11]. Rising personal debt and financial instability—trends accelerating since the 1970s—have fueled persistent bankruptcy, mortgage defaults, and auto repossessions [12]. Medical costs, job loss, and family breakdowns remain leading causes of personal bankruptcy [13].

For middle-income households, financial vulnerability is widespread. Many lack emergency savings and carry significant debt. Consumer spending on essentials has fallen sharply since the early 1970s—down 21 percent on clothing, 22 percent on food, and 44 percent on major appliances [14]. Even dual-income families often live paycheck to paycheck. In 2023, 37 percent of Americans reported that they could not cover a $400 emergency expense without borrowing or selling assets [15].

Despite being the world's wealthiest country, the United States records the highest poverty rates among developed nations. Limited social safety nets and regressive policies contribute to child poverty rates two to four

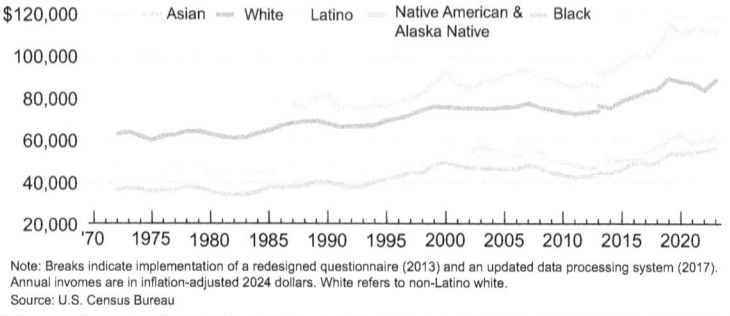

Figure 7.3 *Median household total income by race*

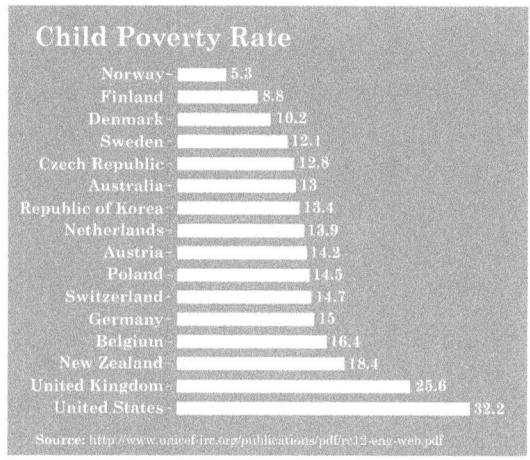

Figure 7.4 *A comparison of child poverty rates among advanced economies*

times higher than the average in peer nations [16]. Debt burdens have grown steadily: the average household now owes $176,000, including $29,000 in auto loans and $17,000 in credit card debt, while student loans affect over 44 million Americans, totaling $1.7 trillion [17].

Median household income has declined in real terms—from $67,673 in 1999 to $62,462 in 2014—while the income threshold for middle-class status has fallen accordingly [18]. The proportion of adults in middle-income households dropped from 55 percent in 2000 to 50 percent in 2014.

Wealth disparities are most noticeable along racial and ethnic lines. White households typically hold 8 to 12 times more wealth than Black households [19]. Over 60 percent of Black and 50 percent of Hispanic households have no financial assets, compared to just 25 percent of White households [20]. Women—particularly single mothers and women of color—also face disproportionate economic pressure due to persistent wage gaps, caregiving responsibilities, and limited opportunities for wealth accumulation [21] (Figures 7.3 and 7.4).

The Economic Inequality Across the World

The distribution of wealth across and within countries remains profoundly unequal. According to the World Bank (2023), countries with a GNI per capita of $13,845 or more are classified as high-income, while those with a GNI per capita of $1,135 or less fall into the low-income category [22]. Despite comprising only about 16 percent of the global population, high-income nations account for more than 55 percent of the world's total income. In contrast, low- and lower-middle-income countries—home to nearly three-quarters of the global population—produce less than 5 percent of global income [22].

Most high-income countries are concentrated in North America, Western Europe, and parts of East Asia, while the poorest countries are primarily located in sub-Saharan Africa and South Asia. One notable exception is China. Over the past four decades, China's rapid economic growth has lifted over 800 million people out of poverty. When China is excluded from global calculations, the trend between 1980 and 2000 shows a sharp increase in international income inequality. During that time, many regions—including Latin America, sub-Saharan Africa, and Eastern Europe—witnessed declines in per capita income, further widening the income gap between nations.

Between 2000 and 2010, global inequality between countries modestly declined due to accelerated economic growth in parts of Asia and Africa. However, despite these relative gains, the absolute income gap between the richest and poorest nations expanded dramatically—from $18,525 in 1980 to nearly $33,000 in 2007 [23]. This absolute divergence remains a persistent feature of the global economy.

Wealth Inequality Among Individuals

At the individual level, global inequality is even more staggering. As of 2023, the wealthiest 1 percent of the world's population owns nearly half of all global assets, while the poorest 50 percent collectively hold just 0.7 percent of global wealth [24]. According to Oxfam's latest inequality report, the top 1 percent have accumulated as much wealth as the bottom 99 percent combined—a trend that has worsened in recent decades.

This concentration of wealth is not an anomaly but a long-term pattern that has intensified across most regions. Between 1988 and 2011, the income of the poorest 10 percent globally rose by less than $3 per year in real terms, while the income of the wealthiest 1 percent surged by more than 180 times [25]. Since the early 1980s, income inequality within countries has increased significantly, including in both developed and emerging economies.

In the United Kingdom, France, India, and China, current levels of income inequality are at or near historic highs. In China, the top 10 percent of earners capture nearly 60 percent of national income, while in India, the top 1 percent hold over 40 percent of total wealth [8]. South Africa, already one of the most unequal societies during apartheid, has become even more unequal in the postapartheid era, with income and wealth disparities remaining deeply entrenched [26].

Moreover, the global financial crisis of 2007–2008 exacerbated inequality. While millions lost jobs, homes, and savings, the wealthiest recovered rapidly and emerged even stronger. In the years following the Great Recession, the global luxury goods market expanded significantly, reflecting the increased purchasing power and resilience of the global elite [27].

Over the past 20 years, the income of the top 1 percent has grown by more than 60 percent globally, compared to stagnation or decline for the majority of the population [8]. This accelerating disparity has sparked growing concern among economists, international organizations, and civil society groups about the social and political consequences of extreme inequality—from declining social mobility and democratic erosion to rising populism and global instability.

Global Economic Inequality: Stark Contrasts and Systemic Disparities

Global economic inequality has reached unprecedented levels. According to Oxfam's 2024 report, just five individuals now possess as much wealth as the poorest half of the world's population—around four billion people [24]. This extreme concentration of wealth reflects both widening disparities between individuals and deep structural inequities embedded in the global economy. The imbalance is evident in striking comparisons: a CEO of an FTSE 100 company can earn in one year what it would take 10,000 garment workers in Bangladesh a lifetime to earn. In Vietnam, a wealthy individual's daily income can match what a poor laborer earns over an entire decade [28].

The human impact of such inequality falls most heavily on women, children, and youth, who are disproportionately concentrated in the lowest income quintiles. In many low- and middle-income countries, exploitative labor practices prevail. Multinational corporations often source cheap labor from vulnerable populations, especially young women in hazardous, low-wage jobs. In Asia's garment sector, the lowest-paid workers are overwhelmingly women and adolescent girls, enduring long hours, unsafe conditions, and minimal legal protection [29].

Over the past four decades, economic inequality has increased in most parts of the world. Transitional and postcommunist societies in Eastern Europe and Central Asia have experienced particularly sharp rises in inequality since the early 1990s [22, 23]. Even within advanced economies, inequality has been rising steadily since the 1970s, driven by technological change, weakened labor protections, and regressive fiscal policies [22].

Globally, the Gini index reveals that inequality today is markedly higher than in the 1980s. Many former Soviet and Eastern European states saw inequality spike between 1990 and 2008 as they transitioned to market economies [8]. Among developing regions, Latin America remains one of the most unequal, despite some reduction in recent years due to redistributive policies in countries such as Brazil and Uruguay. Sub-Saharan Africa also exhibits widespread inequality, with South Africa ranking among the most unequal nations worldwide, characterized by stark racial, geographic, and class divisions [22].

Middle-income countries—which account for much of the world's population growth—frequently face the "middle-income trap," where rapid GDP growth fails to produce inclusive prosperity. Wealth becomes concentrated among urban elites while rural and marginalized populations remain excluded from economic gains. Despite economic globalization and growth in many regions, inequality has widened both between and within countries. Without significant reforms in taxation, labor rights, gender equity, and social protection, the gap between the richest and poorest will deepen, threatening social cohesion and sustainable development.

Causes of Economic Inequality

The persistence and expansion of economic inequality—both globally and within the United States—stem from the complex interaction of political, fiscal, technological, and structural forces. These drivers do not operate in isolation; instead, they reinforce one another, creating a self-perpetuating cycle of wealth concentration and limited upward mobility.

One of the most significant contributors is technological change, which has reshaped labor markets worldwide. Advances in automation, AI, and digital communication have increased demand for highly skilled workers, substantially raising wages for college-educated professionals. At the same time, routine and manual jobs have been displaced or outsourced, pushing down wages for less-educated workers. The rise of digital platforms has enabled a small number of highly skilled professionals to reach global markets and amplify their earnings. At the same time, unskilled labor remains exposed to intense international competition [30].

Globalization has further intensified these pressures. While economic integration has expanded trade and investment flows, it has also accelerated the offshoring of manufacturing jobs from advanced economies to low-wage countries, leading to job insecurity and wage stagnation for less-educated workers [31]. Long-term structural shifts—from agriculture to industry, and later from industry to services—have compounded this trend, as the service sector typically has lower unionization rates and weaker worker protections than manufacturing.

Financial crises add another layer to inequality's persistence. Economic downturns disproportionately harm low- and middle-income households by eroding jobs, savings, and housing wealth. In contrast, wealthy individuals—equipped with liquidity, financial expertise, and access to investment opportunities—often use crises to acquire distressed assets at discounted prices. After the 2008 global financial crisis, for instance, the wealth of the top 1 percent continued to grow at double-digit annual rates [32]. The compounding nature of capital returns entrenches wealth among the already affluent, while debt locks poorer households into cycles of financial vulnerability.

Public policy and fiscal structures have also played a decisive role in widening inequality. In the United States, the top marginal income tax rate has fallen from 70 percent in 1980 to 37 percent in 2023 [33]. Reductions in capital gains, estate, and corporate taxes have shifted the fiscal burden away from the wealthy, while many advanced economies have moved toward less progressive tax systems, weakening redistribution. Cuts to public investment in education, health care, and social safety nets—especially during the Reagan and George W. Bush administrations—have further constrained economic mobility [19]. Rising tuition costs and growing student debt have also limited access to higher education, a key channel for upward mobility.

The decline of organized labor has compounded these trends. Since the early 1980s, union membership has fallen by more than half in both the United States and the United Kingdom [34]. Unions historically played a central role in narrowing wage gaps and securing benefits, job security, and fair compensation. Their erosion has shifted a greater share of income growth toward executives and shareholders. By 2023, the average U.S. CEO earned more than 300 times the pay of the median worker [35].

Corporate power and political influence further shape the landscape of inequality. Large MNCs increasingly determine the direction of tax, trade, and labor policy through extensive lobbying and political contributions. They exploit low-tax jurisdictions, seek regulatory exemptions, and structure supply chains to minimize labor costs [36]. Productivity gains from technological advances are often captured in corporate profits rather than shared with workers, reinforcing the skewed distribution of economic rewards.

Economic inequality also translates into political inequality. Wealthier citizens not only vote at much higher rates but also dominate campaign financing. Nearly 90 percent of Americans in households earning over $75,000 participate in elections, compared to only about 50 percent of those earning under $15,000 [18]. This disparity concentrates political influence among economic elites, reinforcing policy outcomes that favor their interests.

Cultural attitudes shape public tolerance for inequality. In much of Europe, strong welfare traditions foster skepticism toward extreme disparities and support for redistributive measures. In contrast, the United States' political culture, grounded in individualism and meritocracy, often frames wealth as the result of talent and effort. Many Americans view inequality as a natural consequence of market dynamics rather than as a policy failure [37].

Global economic inequality is both a symptom and a cause of more profound systemic disparities in power, opportunity, and political influence. Technological change, globalization, fiscal policy shifts, and corporate dominance interact to sustain and intensify these divides. Without comprehensive reforms—aimed at redistributing resources, strengthening labor rights, and expanding equitable access to education and social protections—inequality will continue to grow, eroding democratic governance and undermining social stability.

The Consequences of Economic Inequality

Economic inequality exerts far-reaching effects on individual well-being, social cohesion, democratic governance, and the overall macroeconomic environment. While moderate disparities can, in theory, incentivize innovation, effort, and entrepreneurship, extreme inequality produces profound social and economic distortions that undermine long-term stability and prosperity.

One common argument in favor of inequality is that market-driven disparities reward talent, hard work, and risk-taking, thereby promoting efficiency and innovation. In this view, unequal outcomes encourage individuals to invest in education, strive for advancement, and pursue entrepreneurial ventures. However, when inequality reaches extreme levels, it erodes equal opportunity and entrenches advantage. As Paul Krugman noted, "a society with highly unequal results is, more or less inevitably, a society with highly unequal opportunity" [38]. In such contexts, success is increasingly determined by inherited privilege rather than merit, and economic advantages translate directly into political influence, market dominance, and preferential access to quality education, further reinforcing entrenched disparities.

The macroeconomic effects of inequality are equally significant. Concentrating wealth at the top suppresses aggregate demand because the marginal propensity to consume is lower among the wealthy than among lower- and middle-income households. By contrast, more equitable income distribution broadens purchasing power, spurring spending, investment, and economic participation [39]. Research has identified several pathways through which inequality contributes to financial instability [40]: suppressed consumer demand, rising household debt and asset bubbles, reliance on debt-led growth strategies, and increased financial speculation by the wealthy. When wages stagnate for large segments of the population, households often rely on credit to maintain living standards. This pattern proved unsustainable in the lead-up to the 2008 financial crisis, when excessive borrowing helped trigger systemic collapse.

The political implications are equally troubling. Excessive concentrations of wealth enable the affluent to exert disproportionate influence over democratic institutions. Through campaign financing, lobbying, and control of media narratives, the ultrarich can shape legislation and policy priorities in their favor. In the United States, for example, the Koch brothers' political spending significantly shaped the Republican Party agenda and the rise of the Tea Party movement [41]. In some cases, wealthy individuals bypass influence channels altogether and enter politics directly, a phenomenon observed in countries ranging from the United States to India, Italy, and Russia. Such trends risk transforming democracy into a plutocracy, where policy reflects monetary influence rather than the electorate's collective will. The effect is even more pronounced in developing countries, where weaker institutions and endemic corruption allow elites to dominate political life with minimal checks.

On a societal level, inequality corrodes social cohesion and reduces mobility. High disparities in income and wealth foster alienation, resentment, and social fragmentation, weakening collective identity and the capacity for cooperative action. Comparative research shows that social mobility is markedly lower in more unequal societies. Ironically, the "American Dream" is now more attainable in egalitarian countries such as Denmark or Sweden than in the United States [42]. Inequality also correlates with higher rates of crime, gun violence, obesity, and mental illness. Unequal societies tend to perform worse across a wide range of health and social indicators—not only for people with low incomes but across all income groups [43].

Economic inequality also undermines public services and fiscal capacity. Extreme wealth allows the rich to secure superior education, health care, and legal representation, while the poor must rely on underfunded public systems. Moreover, many wealthy individuals and corporations exploit offshore tax havens, shell companies, and legal loopholes to minimize their tax obligations. The IMF estimates that more than $7.6 trillion—about 8 percent of global financial wealth—is held offshore, much of it untaxed [44]. This loss of revenue weakens public finances, prompting governments to reduce social spending or shift the tax burden onto the middle class. Underinvestment in infrastructure, public health, and education further entrenches inequality over time.

The effects extend to health and the environment. More unequal societies suffer from higher rates of infectious disease, cardiovascular illness, mental health disorders, and shorter life expectancy. In contrast, egalitarian societies consistently report better health outcomes across all social strata [26]. Inequality also shapes environmental outcomes: the wealthiest individuals have disproportionately large carbon footprints, while low-income communities bear the brunt of pollution, environmental degradation, and climate-related risks. Societies with lower inequality are more likely to implement strong environmental regulations and foster public support for sustainability initiatives [22].

Ultimately, the most profound consequence of extreme inequality is its threat to democratic stability. A broad and secure middle class is the cornerstone of a resilient democracy, providing both the economic foundation and civic engagement necessary to uphold democratic norms. When the majority of citizens lack economic security, the political cost of repression for elites diminishes, and democratic institutions become more vulnerable to erosion. Without policies that reduce inequality and restore broad-based opportunity, the balance between economic power and democratic governance will continue to tilt toward the former, with destabilizing consequences for societies worldwide.

The Plutocrats: The Rise of the Global Superrich

Beyond the wealthiest 1 percent exists an even more exclusive echelon: the global superrich, or plutocrats. Representing roughly 0.1 percent of the global population, this group of billionaires commands an extraordinary share of the world's wealth. The number of billionaires climbed from 2,565 in 2023 to 2,769 in 2024—an addition of 204 new billionaires (Table 7.1). Combined wealth of billionaires leapt from $13 trillion to $15 trillion—a $2 trillion increase in just one year [24]. What distinguishes the superrich is not only the scale of their fortunes, but the speed at which their wealth expands—often outpacing global economic growth. This issue has created a widening divide not simply between the rich and the poor, but between the rich and the ultrarich. While the average income of the top 1 percent is around 15 times higher than that of the bottom 90 percent, the average earnings of the top 0.1 percent exceed those of the bottom 90 percent by more than 120 times [8].

Table 7.1 The list of the wealthiest people in 2025

Rank	Name	Net Worth	Title/Role	Primary Source of Wealth
1	Elon Musk	~$401 B	CEO and Founder (Tesla, SpaceX, xAI, X)	Electric vehicles, space and AI ventures
2	Larry Ellison	~$300 B	Cofounder and CTO, Oracle	Enterprise software and cloud computing
3	Mark Zuckerberg	~$260–267 B	CEO, Meta Platforms	Social media and advertising

(Continues)

Table 7.1 The list of the wealthiest people in 2025 (Continued)

Rank	Name	Net Worth	Title/Role	Primary Source of Wealth
4	Jeff Bezos	~$230–243 B	Founder and Exec. Chair, Amazon	E-commerce, cloud services, media
5	Larry Page	~$156–182 B	Cofounder, Google/Alphabet	Internet search and advertising
6	Jensen Huang	~$152–155 B	CEO, NVIDIA	AI and graphics chips
7	Sergey Brin	~$149 B	Cofounder, Google/Alphabet	Internet search and advertising
8	Steve Ballmer	~$147–178 B	Former CEO, Microsoft	Software, enterprise tech
9	Warren Buffett	~$142–160 B	Chairman and CEO, Berkshire Hathaway	Investments, insurance, and manufacturing
10	Bernard Arnault	~$139–151 B	Chairman and CEO, LVMH	Luxury retail (fashion, cosmetics)
11	Michael Dell	~$128 B	Founder and Chairman, Dell Technologies	Personal computers and enterprise tech
12	Rob Walton	~$118 B	Walmart heir and board member	Retail (Walmart)
13	Jim Walton	~$116 B	Walmart heir and board member	Retail (Walmart)
14	Bill Gates	~$116 B	Cofounder, Microsoft and philanthropist	Software, technology
15	Amancio Ortega	~$111 B	Founder, Zara/Inditex	Fast fashion retail
16	Alice Walton	~$108 B	Walmart heiress	Retail (Walmart)
17	Mukesh Ambani	~$105 B	Chairman, Reliance Industries	Energy, petrochemicals, telecom
18	Michael Bloomberg	~$105 B	Founder, Bloomberg LP and former NYC Mayor	Financial media and terminals
19	Carlos Slim Helu	~$95 B	Telecom mogul (Mexico)	Telecommunications, banking
20	Françoise Bettencourt Meyers	~$80 B	L'Oréal heiress	Cosmetics and beauty (L'Oréal)

Source: Compiled by the authors.

The Global Geography of Billionaire Wealth

The geographic distribution of billionaires reflects both the enduring dominance of Western economies and the rise of emerging markets. Nearly half reside in the United States, while the rest are concentrated in Western Europe, China, and high-growth economies such as Brazil, Mexico, India, Russia, and Saudi Arabia. According to Forbes' 2025 Billionaires List, there are now more than 3,028 billionaires worldwide with a combined net worth exceeding $16.1 trillion—a sharp increase from $8 trillion in 2020 [45]. Europe alone counts more than 450 billionaires, concentrated in Germany, the United Kingdom, and France. While their sources of wealth vary, much of it derives from technological innovation, financial engineering, and regulatory arbitrage, rather than from traditional productive enterprise alone.

The global plutocracy is far from homogenous. It encompasses Silicon Valley technocrats, Wall Street financiers, Russian oligarchs, and multinational corporate executives. In the United States, more than 40 percent of individuals earning over $30 million annually work in finance or corporate management [35]. Many have leveraged digital transformation, first-mover advantages, and global capital flows to amass unprecedented control over information networks, infrastructure, and labor markets.

A central factor in their rise is rent-seeking—the accumulation of wealth through access, privilege, and policy manipulation rather than through productive innovation. In Mexico, Carlos Slim built much of his fortune by capitalizing on privatization policies and monopolistic control over telecommunications. In the United States, hedge fund managers, CEOs, and corporate lawyers often exploit regulatory loopholes and financial asymmetries to maximize personal gain. Similar dynamics are visible in emerging markets such as India, Brazil, Russia, and China, where weak institutions, opaque privatization processes, and limited regulatory oversight create fertile ground for politically connected plutocrats.

The global plutocracy consists of highly educated, internationally mobile elites embedded in dense networks of finance, academia, politics, and philanthropy. Many are alums of prestigious universities and sit on corporate boards, think tanks, and political advisory bodies. Their philanthropic initiatives—often described as efforts to promote "human progress" or "social impact"—not only burnish their reputations but also extend their influence into public policy and cultural agendas.

Prominent foundations such as the Bill & Melinda Gates Foundation, the Chan Zuckerberg Initiative, and the Open Society Foundations have reshaped debates on global health, education, human rights, and media. These organizations direct billions of dollars toward pressing social issues, but they also act as instruments of soft power. By funding policy priorities and setting research agendas, they allow wealthy individuals to steer public discourse outside the bounds of democratic accountability [46]. Mark Zuckerberg and Priscilla Chan's 2015 pledge to donate 99 percent of their Facebook shares remains a landmark case: hailed by admirers as a bold philanthropic gesture but criticized by skeptics as a mechanism for tax avoidance, governance bypass, and the privatization of policymaking. Jeff Bezos has directed billions from his Bezos Earth Fund toward climate initiatives, yet critics argue that such efforts distract from Amazon's own carbon footprint and labor practices. Elon Musk's philanthropic ventures in education and AI safety are often overshadowed by concerns about his growing influence over global communication platforms such as X (formerly Twitter) and satellite infrastructure via Starlink. Similarly, in 2024, Gautam Adani pledged significant investments in health and education programs across India even as his conglomerate faced scrutiny for alleged financial opacity and environmental violations. These cases illustrate how philanthrocapitalism enables billionaires to define the terms of social progress while consolidating their influence.

A Threat to Democracy and Social Stability

As billionaire wealth expands, so does the ability of the superrich to shape political outcomes, regulatory frameworks, and media narratives. Many plutocrats finance electoral campaigns, lobby for favorable legislation, and control major news outlets. In the United States, billionaires like Michael Bloomberg and Peter Thiel have poured vast sums into politics, reinforcing concerns about the erosion of democratic accountability. Globally, the phenomenon is equally visible: in India, tycoons maintain close ties with political elites; in the Philippines, dynastic billionaires dominate both business and government; in Lebanon, wealthy families anchor a clientelist system; and in Russia, oligarchs remain tightly interwoven with state power.

This convergence of economic and political power undermines institutional trust and entrenches inequality. As Thomas Piketty warns, the unchecked accumulation of capital risks giving rise to "patrimonial capitalism," in which wealth and power become hereditary, passed down through dynasties rather than earned through innovation or productivity [47]. The normalization of such inequality threatens to hollow out the middle class, fuel populist discontent, and destabilize fragile democracies. Populist movements in Europe, the United States, and Latin America have surged by exploiting public resentment toward elites perceived as detached and self-serving. Meanwhile, in Africa, billionaires' growing involvement in electoral politics—such as in Nigeria and Kenya—raises fears of democracy being subordinated to plutocratic interests.

The ascent of the superrich raises urgent questions about governance, taxation, and the role of private wealth in public life. While many plutocrats have funded breakthroughs in technology, medicine, and development, others have built fortunes through financial speculation, resource extraction, or regulatory manipulation. What unites them is an unparalleled capacity to shape markets, public policy, and cultural values in ways that often reinforce their own power.

Without strong democratic institutions, transparent taxation systems, and practical constraints on private power, the global plutocracy will continue to operate beyond meaningful accountability. As their influence extends from the economy into politics, education, media, and public values, they are emerging not only as an economic class but also as a new form of global sovereignty—one that challenges the foundations of democratic governance and equitable development.

Persistent Myths About Markets and Inequality

Public debates on markets, wealth, and inequality are often shaped by enduring myths that obscure the structural forces behind economic outcomes. These narratives not only misrepresent reality but also shape policies in ways that entrench existing disparities. A closer examination of the evidence reveals a more complex picture—one in which robust institutions, fair rules, and equitable access to opportunity are indispensable for sustainable prosperity.

One common belief is the idea that markets are always self-correcting and government intervention is inherently distortive. In practice, markets function within rules designed, enforced, and adapted by governments. Without oversight, powerful actors can manipulate prices, form cartels, or grow so large that their collapse would threaten the entire economy—leaving the public to absorb the costs. The 2008 global financial crisis and the multitrillion-dollar rescue packages in the United States and EU, along with the extensive liquidity facilities deployed during the COVID-19 pandemic, illustrate that stable capitalism depends on regulation, state backstops, and antitrust enforcement [44]. Oversight in sectors such as finance, health care, telecommunications, and infrastructure is essential to protect small competitors and vulnerable consumers alike.

Another persistent myth is that extreme inequality is simply the product of hard work and talent. While moderate income differences can indeed reward effort and innovation, today's extreme concentration of wealth is more often the result of market power, inheritance, preferential tax rules, and political influence. In the United States, more than half of billionaire wealth is tied to capital gains—taxed at significantly lower rates than wages [33]. Cross-national evidence shows that as inequality rises, intergenerational mobility declines, undermining the idea that anyone can easily work their way to the top [42]. When economic power becomes political power—through campaign donations, lobbying, or media ownership—the system further entrenches privilege and closes off opportunity.

A third myth holds that the sole purpose of business is to maximize profits for shareholders. While profitability is essential for survival, long-term business success also depends on healthy workforces, reliable supply chains, and resilient communities. Research on "stakeholder capitalism" shows that companies paying living wages, respecting labor rights, and investing in environmental sustainability tend to outperform their peers over time. Conversely, rent-seeking practices—such as excessive share buybacks, regulatory arbitrage, or union suppression—extract value rather than create it, widening the income gap and eroding public trust in markets.

Closely related is the claim that wealth creation is not a zero-sum game and that everyone can get rich. While economic growth can increase total income, access to its gains is far from evenly distributed. Wealth, which generates returns faster than wages rise, tends to concentrate in the hands of capital owners. As assets such as housing, land, and natural resources are finite, gains for the wealthy can come at the expense of those priced out of ownership or burdened with debt [8]. In practice, a "rising tide" does not lift all boats when many households lack the means to participate in wealth accumulation at all.

Another enduring misconception is that race, gender, and geography no longer matter, and inequality is purely an individual issue. In reality, structural barriers remain powerful determinants of economic outcomes. In 2023, the median wealth of single U.S. women was just 55 percent of that of single men, while the typical Black household held one-tenth the wealth of the average white household [12] (Figure 7.5). Wage gaps, occupational segregation, unequal school quality, and discriminatory lending practices continue to limit the ability of women and minorities to turn education and hard work into lasting assets. Globally, women still earn around 20 percent less than men for equivalent work [48]. Inequality is therefore not merely a matter of personal effort but is profoundly shaped by historical legacies and institutional disadvantage.

These myths persist for several reasons. Ideologically, they provide a convenient narrative that blames poverty on individual failings while absolving elites from scrutiny. Politically, they foster policy paralysis—if markets are assumed to be infallible, progressive taxation, stronger labor

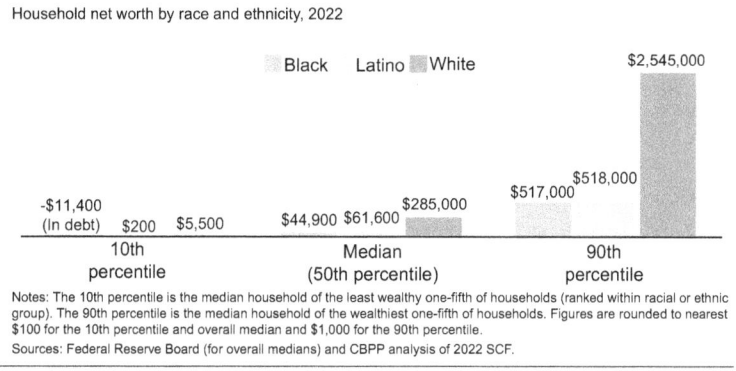

Household net worth by race and ethnicity, 2022

Black   Latino   White

$2,545,000

-$11,400
(In debt) $200 $5,500 $44,900 $61,600 $285,000 $517,000 $518,000

| 10th percentile | Median (50th percentile) | 90th percentile |

Notes: The 10th percentile is the median household of the least wealthy one-fifth of households (ranked within racial or ethnic group). The 90th percentile is the median household of the wealthiest one-fifth of households. Figures are rounded to nearest $100 for the 10th percentile and overall median and $1,000 for the 90th percentile.
Sources: Federal Reserve Board (for overall medians) and CBPP analysis of 2022 SCF.

CENTER ON BUDGET AND POLICY PRIORITIES | CBPP.ORG

Figure 7.5 Wealth is distributed along racial lines

protections, and antitrust enforcement are dismissed as "interference." Democratically, they enable the wealthy to translate economic dominance into political influence under the guise of meritocratic success.

Debunking these myths is not about vilifying success. Instead, it is about recognizing that prosperous, innovative economies rely on robust institutions, fair rules, and broad access to opportunity—not on laissez-faire assumptions that mask structural inequities. By confronting these misconceptions, policymakers and citizens alike can better design systems that balance efficiency with equity, ensuring that the benefits of growth are shared more widely across society.

References

[1] Piketty, T., and E. Saez. 2003. "Income Inequality in the United States, 1913–1998." *The Quarterly Journal of Economics* 118, no. 1, pp. 1–41.

[2] DeLong, J.B. 2023. *Slouching Towards Utopia: An Economic History of the Twentieth Century.* Basic Books.

[3] Mishel, L., J. Bivens, E. Gould, and H. Shierholz. 2012. *The State of Working America.* Cornell University Press.

[4] Hacker, J.S., and P. Pierson. 2010. *Winner-Take-all Politics: How Washington Made the Rich Richer--and Turned Its Back on the Middle Class.* Simon and Schuster.

[5] Piketty, T., E. Saez, and G. Zucman. 2018. "Distributional National Accounts: Methods and Estimates for the United States." *The Quarterly Journal of Economics* 133, no. 2, pp. 553–609.

[6] Congressional Budget Office. 2022. The Distribution of Household Income, 2019. https://www.cbo.gov

[7] Economic Policy Institute. 2022. State of Working America Wages Report.

[8] World Inequality Lab. 2023. World Inequality Database. https://wid.world.

[9] Tax Policy Center. 2023. Historical Highest Marginal Income Tax Rates. https://www.taxpolicycenter.org.

[10] Goldin, C.D., and L.F. Katz. 2008. *The Race between Education and Technology.* Harvard University Press.

[11] Center for Retirement Research. 2022. *National Retirement Risk Index Update.* Boston College.

[12] Federal Reserve Bank of New York. 2023. Quarterly Report on Household Debt and Credit.

[13] American Bankruptcy Institute. 2022. Annual Bankruptcy Filings Data.

[14] Bureau of Labor Statistics. 2023. Consumer Expenditure Survey. https://www.bls.gov/cex/.

[15] Federal Reserve. 2023. Consumer Expenditure Survey. https://www.bls.gov/cex/.

[16] UNICEF. 2023. Child Poverty in Rich Countries.

[17] Department of Education. 2023. Federal Student Loan Portfolio.

[18] Pew Research Center. 2022. Middle Class Decline in the United States.

[19] Urban Institute. 2023. Racial Wealth Gap in the United States.

[20] Brookings Institution. 2022. The Black-White Wealth Gap: Why It Exists and How We Can Fix It.

[21] National Women's Law Center. 2023. The State of Women in the US Economy.

[22] World Bank. 2023. World Development Report: Sustainable Growth for All.

[23] Milanovic, B. 2016. *Global Inequality: A New Approach for the Age of Globalization*. Harvard University Press.

[24] Oxfam. 2024. *Inequality Inc.: How Corporations Drive the Wealth Gap*. https://www.oxfam.org.

[25] Lakner, C., and B. Milanovic. 2016. "Global Income Distribution: From the Fall of the Berlin Wall to the Great Recession." *The World Bank Economic Review* 30, no. 2, pp. 203–232.

[26] OECD. 2023. Income Inequality Update. https://www.oecd.org/social/income-distribution-database.htm.

[27] Bain & Company. 2023. Luxury Goods Worldwide Market Study.

[28] James, D., Q. Branch, and D.D. James. 2023. Fair Work Commission.

[29] Clean Clothes Campaign. 2023. Exploitation in the Garment Industry. https://cleanclothes.org.

[30] Horne, R. 2024. "Employment and Social Trends by Region." *World Employment and Social Outlook* 2024, no. 1, pp. 37–60.

[31] Rodrik, D. 2017. Straight Talk on Trade: Ideas for a Sane World Economy.

[32] Saez, E., and G. Zucman. 2019. *The Triumph of Injustice: How the Rich Dodge Taxes and How to Make them Pay*. WW Norton & Company.

[33] Tax Policy Center. 2023. Historical Tax Rates. https://www.taxpolicycenter.org.

[34] Bureau of Labor Statistics (BLS). 2023. Union Membership Summary. https://www.bls.gov.

[35] Economic Policy Institute (EPI). 2023. CEO Pay Continues to Soar.

[36] Stiglitz, J.E. 2019. *People, Power, and Profits: Progressive Capitalism for an Age of Discontent*. Penguin UK.

[37] Alesina, A., and E.L. Glaeser. 2004. *Fighting Poverty in the US and Europe: A World of Difference*. Oxford University Press.

[38] Krugman, P. 2009. *The Conscience of a Liberal*. WW Norton & Company.

[39] Stiglitz, J. 2012. *The Price of Inequality*. W.W. Norton & Company.

[40] Kumhof, M., R. Rancière, and P. Winant. 2015. "Inequality, Leverage, and Crises." *American Economic Review* 105, no. 3, pp. 1217–1245.

[41] Mayer, J. 2016. *Dark Money: The Hidden History of the Billionaires Behind the Rise of the Radical Right*. Vintage.

[42] Corak, M. 2013. "Income Inequality, Equality of Opportunity, and Intergenerational Mobility." *Journal of Economic Perspectives* 27, no. 3, pp. 79–102.

[43] Wilkinson, R.G., and K. Pickett. 2009. *The Spirit Level: Why More Equal Societies Almost Always do Better*, Vol. 6. London: Allen Lane.

[44] International Monetary Fund (IMF). 2022. Fiscal Policy and Income Inequality.

[45] Forbes. 2025. "The World's Billionaires." http://forbes.com/billionaires/list/.

[46] Giridharadas, A. 2019. *Winners Take All: The Elite Charade of Changing the World*. Vintage.

[47] Piketty, T. 2014. *Capital in the Twenty-First Century*. Harvard University Press.

[48] ILO. 2023. World Employment and Social Outlook: Trends.

CHAPTER 8

The Giant Corporations

An Incredible Concentration of Power and Wealth

For much of history, political and economic power was concentrated in the hands of the church and the state, which functioned as the principal centers of decision making [1]. With the rise of modern capitalism in the 18th century, corporations gradually emerged as powerful economic actors, eventually surpassing the influence of religious and state institutions. Initially, corporate expansion was constrained by limited capital accumulation, geographical boundaries, and legal or cultural barriers. However, in the second half of the 19th century, regulatory changes facilitated their rapid growth.

The introduction of limited liability laws protected business owners from personal responsibility for corporate debts, while the development of financial exchanges enabled more efficient interaction between investors and businesses. This flexibility, in turn, accelerated capital accumulation and fueled corporate expansion. While corporate growth remained steady throughout the 20th century, it gained remarkable momentum in the 1990s. The end of the Cold War, the rise of new information technologies, and, above all, globalization provided unprecedented conditions for a dramatic concentration of economic power in a small number of large corporations.

The transformation was significant: in 1980, the world's 1,000 largest corporations generated $2.64 trillion in revenue, employed 21 million people, and had a combined market capitalization of $900 billion. By 2012, their revenues had surged to $34 trillion, their workforce to 73 million, and their market capitalization to $28 trillion [1]. Today, these corporate giants dominate city skylines and command extraordinary accumulations of wealth (Table 8.1).

Table 8.1 The Top 50 largest corporations as of July 2025

Rank	Corporation	Country	Market Capitalization
1	NVIDIA	United States	$4.2T
2	Microsoft	United States	$3.8T
3	Apple	United States	$3.1T
4	Amazon	United States	$2.4T
5	Alphabet	United States	$2.2T
6	Meta Platforms	United States	$1.8T
7	Saudi Aramco	Saudi Arabia	$1.6T
8	Broadcom	United States	$1.3T
9	TSMC	Taiwan	$1.2T
10	Tesla	United States	$1.1T
11	Berkshire Hathaway	United States	$1.0T
12	JPMorgan Chase	United States	$801.5B
13	Walmart	United States	$759.3B
14	Eli Lilly	United States	$694.2B
15	Oracle	United States	$690.9B
16	Visa	United States	$681.5B
17	Tencent	China	$599.2B
18	Netflix	United States	$513.9B
19	Mastercard	United States	$500.9B
20	Exxon Mobil	United States	$464.3B
21	Costco	United States	$421.4B
22	Johnson & Johnson	United States	$394.4B
23	Procter & Gamble	United States	$363.7B
24	Palantir	United States	$360.1B
25	ICBC	China	$359.0B
26	SAP	Germany	$357.2B
27	Home Depot	United States	$356.3B
28	Bank of America	United States	$352.2B
29	AbbVie	United States	$334.7B
30	Samsung	South Korea	$316.1B
31	Coca-Cola	United States	$301.7B
32	Agricultural Bank of China	China	$293.7B
33	ASML	Netherlands	$290.2B
34	Novo Nordisk	Denmark	$289.7B
35	Hermès	France	$288.6B

Rank	Corporation	Country	Market Capitalization
36	Alibaba	China	$286.4B
37	China Construction Bank	China	$283.1B
38	General Electric	United States	$279.0B
39	Philip Morris International	United States	$278.7B
40	LVMH	France	$273.6B
41	Cisco	United States	$269.7B
42	IBM	United States	$265.8B
43	Wells Fargo	United States	$259.4B
44	Roche	Switzerland	$258.9B
45	T-Mobile US	United States	$257.3B
46	UnitedHealth	United States	$256.5B
47	Chevron	United States	$255.2B
48	AMD	United States	$255.1B
49	Nestlé	Switzerland	$254.9B
50	Prosus	Netherlands	$253.1B

Although comparing corporate revenues with national GDPs is not a strictly accurate measure, it provides a striking illustration of corporate influence. The world's 10 largest corporations collectively earn more than the total government revenue of 180 countries, including Ireland, Indonesia, Israel, Colombia, Greece, South Africa, Iraq, and Vietnam [2]. Walmart, ranked as the 10th largest economic entity in the world, is economically larger than major national economies such as Australia, South Korea, and India.

Apple's cash reserves alone exceed the GDPs of nearly two-thirds of the world's countries [3]. In 2020, the largest global corporations included Apple, Saudi Aramco, Amazon, Microsoft, Alphabet, Alibaba, Facebook, Tencent, Berkshire Hathaway, and Taiwan Semiconductor.

Beyond financial metrics, other indicators—such as market share, growth rates, and consumer reach—demonstrate the extraordinary rise of global corporations over the past two decades. Technology companies have grown at an unprecedented speed. Founded in 1998, Google now processes more than 40,000 search queries every second, amounting to over 3.5 billion daily searches and 1.2 trillion annually [4]. Meta (Facebook), founded in 2004, had over 2.85 billion monthly active users as of May 2021—more than the populations of China and the United States combined [5].

Amazon.com, launched in 1995 as an online bookstore, reported net sales of $386 billion in 2020. By June 2021, the market capitalizations of leading tech firms had reached extraordinary levels: Apple at $2 trillion, Amazon at $1.7 trillion, Google's parent company Alphabet at $1.5 trillion, and Facebook at $1 trillion.

Over the past decade, the share of the global economy controlled by large corporations has expanded sharply, while competition from small- and medium-sized enterprises has declined at a similar pace. This feature has allowed a relatively small number of companies to dominate global markets, secure higher profits, and outcompete smaller rivals. The largest technology firms have leveraged their scale to cement market dominance and generate immense revenues.

A handful of companies—typically six to nine—control much of the infrastructure of the information economy, from Internet search and online advertising to e-commerce, cloud computing, and social media. According to the McKinsey Global Institute, just 10 percent of the world's publicly traded companies account for nearly 80 percent of all corporate profits [6]. Corporations with annual revenues exceeding $1 billion generate around 60 percent of total global corporate income [6].

In the United States, the concentration of wealth is particularly pronounced. The share of GDP generated by the 100 largest U.S. companies increased from roughly 33 percent in 1994 to 46 percent in 2013 [6]. Some long-established corporations, such as ExxonMobil, Berkshire Hathaway, Procter & Gamble, Walmart, Pfizer, and Johnson & Johnson, have maintained their positions for decades. Others—Apple, Alphabet, Microsoft, Amazon, and Facebook—are newer entrants that rapidly ascended to global dominance through innovation, mergers, and favorable regulatory environments. While most of these corporate giants originate in the United States, Western Europe, and Japan, influential firms such as Alibaba, ICBC, and China Mobile reflect the growing presence of emerging economies in the global corporate landscape (Table 8.1).

Doing More With Less: More Revenues and Fewer Employees

Traditionally, firms' revenues, market capitalizations, and assets were closely correlated with workforce size—companies with large revenues typically relied on a substantial number of employees and physical assets. Yet, over the past three decades—propelled by globalization and technological innovation—multinational corporations have increasingly done more with less: generating higher revenues with leaner staffing and minimized tangible assets [3].

Today, many high-technology and platform-based firms exemplify this shift. For instance, Meta (Facebook) employed approximately 58,000 people in 2020, yet delivered $86 billion in revenue with a market capitalization of $750 billion. Netflix, with just 9,000 employees, reached a market cap of over $226 billion and nearly $25 billion in revenue that same year.

This "lean but massive" model extends beyond digital natives. Automation, globalized supply chains, and outsourcing have enabled legacy giants such as Nike, Apple, Exxon Mobil, and AT&T to boost productivity while downsizing. Exxon Mobil's workforce, for example, shrank from 150,000 in the 1960s to under 75,000—despite expanding through mergers [6, 7]. Moreover, large American corporations now employ a disproportionate share of low-wage workers—about 66 percent—underscoring how efficiency gains can come at labor's expense [6, 7].

Recent reports highlight an intensifying trend: public companies are streamlining operations through layoffs, especially white-collar roles. A *Wall Street Journal* analysis reveals that over the past three years, U.S. public firms reduced white-collar staffing by roughly 3.5 percent, prioritizing "revenue per employee" as a success metric. Technologies like AI are central, enabling automation of routine tasks while sustaining or increasing revenue. Walmart, for example, grew sales by 40 percent over a decade even as it reduced staffing by 100,000 [8].

CEOs increasingly view workforce reductions as strategic efficiency moves. For example, Wells Fargo and Bank of America have reduced their headcounts dramatically (23 percent and substantial declines since 2010, respectively), citing AI and attrition as tools to create leaner operations [9]. AI-driven job cuts are accelerating across major firms, with Microsoft, Intel, and BT leading the way—prioritizing automation even amid high profits.

Moreover, one in five S&P 500 companies now employs fewer people than a decade ago, with revenue still rising. Firms such as Hewlett Packard Enterprise now operate with their fewest employees since becoming independent. At the same time, Bank of America has shrunk its workforce from 285,000 to approximately 213,000, all while increasing revenues by 18 percent [10]. Managerial and executive roles have also seen declines—managerial roles down 6.1 percent, executives down 4.6 percent between May 2022 and May 2025 [10] (Table 8.2).

Table 8.2 The top 20 companies ranked by revenue per employee in 2025

Rank	Company	Revenue Per Employee
1	SYNNEX (SNEX)	$21.93 M
2	Bio-Techne (BTSG)	$18.78 M
3	Valero Energy (VLO)	$13.08 M
4	RenaissanceRe Holdings (RNR)	$12.33 M
5	Plains All American Pipeline (PAA)	$11.98 M
6	Plains GP Holdings (PAGP)	$11.98 M
7	Phillips 66 (PSX)	$10.84 M
8	AerCap Holdings (AER)	$10.07 M
9	Cheniere Energy (LNG)	$9.20 M
10	World Kinect Corporation (WKC)	$8.91 M
11	PBF Energy (PBF)	$8.59 M
12	Apollo Global Management (APO)	$8.42 M
13	McKesson Corporation (MCK)	$7.98 M
14	Civitas Resources (CIVI)	$7.95 M
15	Marathon Petroleum (MPC)	$7.57 M
16	EOG Resources (EOG)	$7.45 M
17	Enterprise Products Partners (EPD)	$7.14 M
18	Antero Resources (AR)	$7.02 M
19	Chord Energy (CHRD)	$6.89 M
20	Sunoco LP (SUN)	$6.88 M

Source: The Authors.

Platform companies such as Uber and Airbnb exemplify how to generate massive revenues with minimal traditional assets. As of 2024, Uber had approximately 31,100 employees but generated $43.9 billion in revenue—an 18 percent year-over-year increase. Its mobility, delivery, and freight segments collectively generated the revenue with comparatively lean staffing [11]. The company also launched a $20 billion stock buyback in 2025 to reward shareholders [12]. In 2024, Airbnb had only around 7,300 employees but pulled in $11.1 billion in revenue—a 12.1 percent increase year-over-year [11]. In Q2 2025, the firm beat forecasts with $3.1 billion in revenue (up 13%), while projecting Q3 revenue between $4.02 and $4.10 billion. Despite these figures, its stock dipped due to margin pressures from new investments and regulatory challenges. Airbnb reaffirmed its full-year adjusted EBITDA margin target of at least 34.5 percent [13].

Meanwhile, broader gig economy trends show platform-based companies employing fewer traditional staff yet tapping into millions of independent contractors—for example, Uber and Lyft collectively engage over 2 million U.S. drivers. While corporations streamline operations and bolster profitability, the human costs are significant. Layoffs, reduced management, and AI-driven automation are shrinking job security, narrowing advancement opportunities, and eroding worker morale. These efficiency gains—often foregrounding shareholder returns—pose growing challenges to traditional employment structures and labor well-being [14].

The Winner-Take-All Capitalism

Large corporations increasingly benefit from immense financial, technological, and managerial resources, giving them powerful competitive edges over smaller rivals. In tech, giants such as Google, Microsoft, Meta, and Amazon have become so dominant that competition from small- and mid-sized firms is severely constrained [6]. This dynamic is further entrenched by network effects, where platforms improve exponentially with greater user scale, reinforcing monopolistic tendencies.

In the financial sector, consolidation has surged. As of Q1 2025, the four largest U.S. banks—JPMorgan Chase, Bank of America, Citigroup, and Wells Fargo—collectively hold a staggering share of industry assets. JPMorgan alone controls approximately $3.64 trillion, followed by Bank of America with about $2.62 trillion and Citigroup with $1.76 trillion. Globally, the top 10 banks manage nearly half of the worldwide assets under management [15].

This pattern of consolidation spans numerous U.S. industries—from aviation and telecommunications to pharmaceuticals, media, and insurance—and is mirrored in Europe and Asia, driven by global logistics and production capacities.

To minimize tax liabilities, many large corporations employ complex financial engineering. UNCTAD notes that the top 100 firms often have an average of 20 holding companies and over 500 affiliates, frequently based in low-tax jurisdictions [7]. For example, in 2015, Apple used Irish subsidiaries—without local employees—to report most of its foreign profits, resulting in extremely low effective tax rates—about 0.005 percent on European profits [16, 17].

Size also brings political power. Leading companies across sectors—such as General Electric (GE), Boeing, Comcast, FedEx, Amazon, Pfizer, and Google—rank among the top spenders on lobbying [18]. Oxfam has documented that over 140 multinational corporations use political connections to influence global and national policymaking [19]. U.S. corporations spend around $2.6 billion annually on lobbying, often hiring former government officials and supplementing their efforts with professional lobbyists to shape regulations in their favor [7]. This lobbying machine is not unique to the United States: Brussels alone hosts over 30,000 corporate lobbyists shaping EU policy for over 500 million consumers [7].

Operationally, global giants leverage outsourcing and supply chain flexibility to move across borders with minimal capital investment. This agility allows them to skirt responsibility for labor or environmental standards and pit nations against each other for concessions—such as tax breaks or labor restrictions. For instance, Malaysia attracted semiconductor manufacturing through labor union bans and tax incentives [6].

Acquisitions are another strategy. In 2020, Apple held roughly $200 billion in cash, enabling it to absorb downturns and invest in innovation.

Facebook's acquisitions of Instagram (2012) and WhatsApp (2014) for $1 billion and $22 billion, respectively, eliminated major competitive threats. GE also develops health care products in low-cost markets like India to exploit regional advantages in talent and cost [7].

These strategies have reshaped market dynamics, eliminating mid-sized competitors. Major examples include the decline of Nokia, Motorola, and BlackBerry, partly attributable to competitive pressure from Apple. Overall, McKinsey finds the average tenure of companies in the S&P 500 has dropped dramatically—from 61 years in 1958 to 18 years by 2011—as firms are displaced by more adaptable giants [7].

The Decline of Small Business and the Rise of Corporate Concentration

Over the past four decades, the United States has witnessed a sustained and significant decline in small business activity, coinciding with the rapid expansion of large MNCs and their growing dominance over markets. Between 1980 and 2012, the number of small construction firms fell by 15,000, and more than 70,000 small manufacturers disappeared, according to the U.S. Economic Census (1997–2012). Local retailers experienced an even sharper contraction, losing 108,000 establishments—a 40 percent decline relative to population [20]. This contraction has occurred across multiple sectors, including retail, banking, agriculture, and food processing.

In the 1980s, local retailers accounted for nearly half of consumer goods sold in U.S. stores. Today, that share has dropped to about one-quarter [21]. Similarly, the proportion of total business revenue generated by firms with fewer than 100 employees declined by over 20 percent between 1997 and 2012 [22]. As small enterprises contract, large corporations have consolidated control over an increasing share of economic activity, fundamentally reshaping market structures.

Despite the appearance of variety on supermarket shelves and in shopping centers, much of the consumer market is controlled by a small number of parent corporations. For example, a single eyewear conglomerate manufactures nearly every major sunglass brand globally

[27]. The beef, beer, and dairy industries are also highly concentrated, with a few dominant companies controlling the majority of production and distribution [21].

Retail is among the most visibly concentrated sectors. Walmart now captures one in every four dollars Americans spend on groceries and holds the majority market share in over half of grocery sales across 40 metropolitan areas [21]. The online retail landscape is even more consolidated: in 2015, Amazon accounted for 51 percent of all growth in online spending and controlled nearly 49 percent of the U.S. e-commerce market. By 2023, Amazon's dominance had grown further, accounting for nearly 38 percent of total U.S. e-commerce sales, with its logistics network expanding into physical retail, cloud computing, and advertising.

Regulatory changes have facilitated this consolidation. In 2010, the Department of Justice raised the threshold for defining industry concentration, making it easier for mergers and acquisitions to proceed without antitrust challenges [21]. Nevertheless, *The Wall Street Journal* reported that one-third of U.S. industries still qualify as highly concentrated under federal criteria. Consolidation now spans aviation, telecommunications, pharmaceuticals, technology, agriculture, and food production—raising barriers to entry for new firms.

The Brookings Institution notes that new business formation rates have dropped sharply over recent decades. More troubling, business closures now outpace start-ups across all 50 states and in more than 360 U.S. metropolitan areas. This reversal marks not only a slowdown in entrepreneurship but also a weakening of local economic ecosystems and community resilience.

While globalization and technological change have played roles in this shift, the deeper causes are structural and political. Since the Reagan administration, federal policies have increasingly favored large corporations through deregulation, weakened antitrust enforcement, and tax structures that disadvantage smaller firms. Rather than challenging monopoly power, policymakers have often enabled it—creating a marketplace where dominant firms can suppress competition, depress wages, raise consumer prices, and reduce product diversity.

Large MNCs wield advantages that small businesses cannot match: global supply chains, sophisticated lobbying networks, access to cheap capital, and economies of scale that lower costs and improve margins. In contrast, small and family-owned enterprises operate in a regulatory and financial environment designed for corporate giants, limiting their ability to grow and compete.

The decline of small businesses has profound economic and societal implications. Small firms have historically been engines of job creation, middle-class prosperity, and community development. They distribute wealth more locally, support civic engagement, and foster competitive markets that check excessive corporate power. As small businesses vanish, wealth and influence become increasingly concentrated, eroding not just economic diversity but also democratic pluralism and the rule of law.

Eroding State Sovereignty and Diluting Nationhood

Large MNCs increasingly leverage the global economic system to their advantage while exerting substantial influence over national policies. For governments—especially those seeking FDI, job creation, and economic growth—attracting MNCs can be essential. Their presence can generate tax revenues that help fund political programs and infrastructure projects. However, this dependency comes at a cost: once embedded in a host economy, large corporations often gain the leverage to shape national agendas in their favor [23–25].

MNCs rarely need to resort to corrupt or illegal practices to secure concessions. For economically vulnerable states, the mere threat of a corporation relocating investments and operations elsewhere can be enough to sway policy [26, 28]. Suppose a government revokes a permit or imposes unfavorable regulations. In that case, an MNC can swiftly transfer assets to a more accommodating jurisdiction, leaving the host country to face job losses, capital flight, and economic disruption.

Structural advantages give corporations an edge over nation-states. They are inherently mobile, motivated by profit rather than national loyalty, and—thanks to globalization and advances in technology—are largely unconstrained by territorial, legal, or cultural boundaries [29]. Once granted market access, MNCs often extend their influence beyond economics into political, social, and cultural arenas. Their financial

clout enables them to lobby for legislative changes, influence regulatory frameworks, and promote policies aligned with their commercial
interests. They also engage in public service provision—such as health
care, education, and infrastructure—activities framed as CSR but often
serving to entrench market access and influence. In weaker states, such
influence may be used to secure resource concessions, weaken labor protections, or evade environmental standards in the name of efficiency or
philanthropy.

Recent examples underscore this dynamic. In 2020, the EU ordered
Apple to pay €13 billion in back taxes to Ireland after ruling that its
tax arrangements constituted illegal state aid. Apple had routed the vast
majority of its non-U.S. profits through Irish subsidiaries that paid an
effective tax rate as low as 0.005 percent in some years, highlighting how
corporate tax strategies can undermine national sovereignty over fiscal
policy. Similarly, Amazon's high-profile disputes with U.S. labor regulators and European courts—over unionization drives, warehouse safety,
and alleged anticompetitive practices—illustrate how MNCs can resist
domestic regulatory authority. In 2021, Amazon successfully pressured
local governments in New York and Virginia to offer billions in tax breaks
and infrastructure commitments in exchange for siting corporate offices,
showing how competition among jurisdictions can be exploited to secure
favorable terms.

The growing influence of MNCs poses a direct challenge to state sovereignty. By fragmenting political authority and blurring the boundaries
between governance and market activity, they weaken the state's capacity
to perform core functions. Even when states remain the primary formal
actors in the international system, their ability to safeguard property
rights, maintain monetary stability, enforce contracts, and protect the
environment is increasingly constrained by corporate power [30].

This feature marks a sharp departure from the mid-20th-century
model of corporate-state alignment. In the 1950s, General Motors President Charles Wilson famously declared, "What was good for our country
was good for General Motors and vice versa" [15]. Today, corporate and
national interests have diverged. Leading firms such as Apple, Walmart,
Amazon, Unilever, and BlackRock determine operational locations and
staffing strategies based on shareholder returns rather than national

priorities. Many of the largest U.S. corporations—including Apple, IBM, Microsoft, and GE—have offshored jobs, shifted profits to low-tax jurisdictions, and accumulated vast reserves beyond the reach of domestic taxation.

In this emerging global order, the dominant principle is not national sovereignty but profit maximization. By prioritizing shareholder value over public interest and extending operations beyond the effective juris-diction of any single government, large corporations are not only eroding state sovereignty but also diluting the very concept of nationhood in the 21st-century political economy.

Aggravating Economic Inequality

Large MNCs contribute to the deepening of economic inequality in multiple, interrelated ways. While corporate profitability has soared over recent decades, the distribution of these gains has been heavily skewed toward top executives and shareholders, leaving ordinary workers with marginal benefits. For S&P 500 companies, the average CEO-to-worker pay ratio soared to 285:1 in 2024, with CEOs earning an average of $18.9 million, while the median worker made around $66,300—reflecting a 7 percent rise in CEO compensation compared to minimal gains for employees [31]. Within the S&P 500, the median CEO-to-worker pay ratio stood at 192:1, and across the Equilar 100 companies, it ballooned to 300:1.

Through political influence and lobbying, many corporations secure favorable regulations and reduced tax rates that disproportionately benefit the affluent at the expense of the broader public. This dynamic shifts a heavier relative tax burden onto average citizens, while corporate elites— often labeled "crony capitalists"—continue to accumulate wealth and consolidate power.

Corporate consolidation over the past two decades has amplified these disparities. As profits have grown, large corporations have directed unprecedented sums toward stock repurchase programs. These buybacks inflate share prices, disproportionately benefiting wealthy investors and executives, whose compensation packages are often heavily weighted toward stock options. S&P 500 companies executed $795 billion in buybacks in 2023—a dip from the 2022 peak of $923 billion—but repurchases rebounded strongly in early 2024, totaling $472 billion in the first half—a 21 percent increase over the same period the previous year [32].

In the technology sector in particular, equity-based pay comprises a substantial portion of executive compensation, resulting in sharp income gains for corporate leaders. At the same time, wage growth for average employees remains stagnant. Maximizing returns to shareholders effectively means allocating a greater share of short-term profits to those who already hold substantial wealth. Meta Platforms led the charge in early 2024, announcing a $50 billion buyback plan as part of its "Year of Efficiency," reflecting renewed confidence among tech giants in prioritizing shareholder returns [33].

Technology giants, often operating with limited competition, have consistently reported some of the highest profit margins in the corporate world. Their business models allow them to generate immense revenues with comparatively small workforces. As shown in Table 8.2, per-employee revenue of many S&P500 companies exceeded US$5 million. Cutting corporate tax rates for such firms tends to disproportionately benefit high-income individuals while doing little to alleviate inequality. Empirical evidence suggests that corporate tax cuts are a significant driver of rising income inequality [34].

MNCs have also played a pivotal role in eroding organized labor in the United States. Since the 1980s, many large corporations have actively resisted unionization, shifting production to nonunion facilities or outsourcing to low-cost countries. By 2013, U.S. union density had fallen to just 11 percent. Research consistently shows that unions are critical in fostering shared prosperity and lowering income inequality.

The excessive concentration of wealth carries broader macroeconomic risks. When wealth is more evenly distributed, a larger proportion of the population possesses spending power, stimulating demand, economic growth, and further wealth creation. By contrast, extreme inequality depresses consumption, hampers growth, and can even contribute to financial instability. When a substantial share of the population lacks sufficient income, households increasingly rely on debt to meet basic needs. Rising debt burdens, in turn, heighten the risk of systemic financial crises [35].

Beyond economics, extreme inequality undermines social cohesion and reduces social mobility. It correlates with a range of sociocultural problems, including higher rates of crime, gun violence, mental illness, obesity, and other health issues [36]. Societies with severe economic disparities tend to exhibit greater levels of fear, mistrust, and social division. Empirical studies further reveal that inequality negatively affects the health and well-being of people across all income levels. For instance, countries with high income inequality report elevated risks of infectious diseases and cardiovascular conditions [36]. The deepening of economic inequality—fueled in part by the structural practices of large MNCs—undermines both economic stability and societal well-being, leaving more people living in insecurity and fewer with genuine prospects for upward mobility.

References

[1] Serafeim, G. 2013. *The Role of the Corporation in Society: An Alternative View and Opportunities for Future Research*. Harvard Business School.

[2] Wheelwright, G. September 25, 2016. "What are the Big Tech Companies Lobbying for this Election?" *The Guardian Website*. https://theguardian.com/technology/2016/sep/26/tech-news-lobby-election-taxes-tpp-national-security.

[3] Khanna, P., and I.B.E. Rodriguez. 2016. "These 25 Companies Are More Powerful Than Many Countries." *Foreign Policy*, March/April.

[4] http://internetlivestats.com/google-search-statistics/.

[5] https://zephoria.com/top-15-valuable-facebook-statistics/.

[6] The Economist. 2016. The Rise of the Superstars, Special Report, September 17th, 2016.

[7] Hardoon, D., R. Fuentes-Nieva, and S. Ayele. 2016. *An Economy For the 1%: How Privilege and Power in the Economy Drive Extreme Inequality and How this can be Stopped*. Oxfam.

[8] The Wall Street Journal. The Biggest Companies Across America Are Cutting Their Workforces. https://www.wsj.com/business/the-biggest-companies-across-america-are-cutting-their-workforces-a0e8739a?utm_source=chatgpt.com.

[9]   The Wall Street Journal. CEOs Are Shrinking Their Workforces—and They Couldn't Be Prouder. https://www.wsj.com/lifestyle/careers/layoff-business-strategy-reduce-staff-11796d66?utm_source=chatgpt.com.

[10]   Human Resources Director. Why Fewer Workers Add up to More Growth for Corporate America: Report. https://www.hcamag.com/us/news/general/why-fewer-workers-add-up-to-more-growth-for-corporate-america-report/539602?utm_source=chatgpt.com.

[11]   Wikipedia Uber. 2025. https://en.wikipedia.org/wiki/Uber?utm_source=chatgpt.com.

[12]   Airbnb Expects Slower Growth in Second Half of 2025. *Shares Fall*. https://www.reuters.com/business/airbnb-expects-slower-growth-second-half-2025-shares-fall-2025-08-06/?utm_source=chatgpt.com.

[13]   Airbnb Growth Accelerates as Q2 Earnings Beat. Why The Stock Is Falling Anyway. https://www.investors.com/news/technology/airbnb-stock-abnb-q2-2025-earnings-news/?utm_source=chatgpt.com.

[14]   The Wall Street Journal. 2025. "The Biggest Companies Across America are Cutting Their Workforces." https://www.wsj.com/business/the-biggest-companies-across-america-are-cutting-their-workforces-a0e8739a?utm_source=chatgpt.com.

[15]   Cerny, P.G. 1995. "Globalization and the Changing Logic of Collective Action." *International Organization* 49, no. 4, pp. 595–625.

[16]   Allison, C., E. Fleisje, W. Glevey, and W.L. Johannes. 2014. *Trends and Key Drivers of Income Inequality*. Marshall Economic Research Group, University of Cambridge.

[17]   Berrill, J., and G. Mannella. 2013. "Are Firms from Developed Markets More International than Firms from Emerging Markets?." *Research in International Business and Finance* 27, no. 1, pp. 147–161.

[18]   Roach, B. 2007. *Corporate Power in a Global Economy*. Global Development and Environment Institute, Tufts University, 1–36.

[19]   Greider, W. 1998. *One World, Ready or Not: The Manic Logic of Global Capitalism*. Simon and Schuster.

[20]   Baldwin, W., and J. Scott. 2013. *Market Structure and Technological Change*. Taylor & Francis.

[21]   Mitchell, Mitchell, S. 2016. "The View from the Shop—Antitrust and the Decline of America's Independent Businesses." *The Antitrust Bulletin* 61, no. 4, pp. 498–516.

[22]   US Economic Census. 1997/2012. Available at: www.census.gov/programs-surveys/economic-census.htm

[23]   Detomasi, D. 2015. "The Multinational Corporation as a Political Actor: 'Varieties of Capitalism' Revisited." *Journal of Business Ethics* 128, no. 3, pp. 685–700.

[24] Sassen, S. 1996. *Losing Control?: Sovereignty in the Age of Globalization.* Columbia University Press.

[25] Kobrin, S.J., A.G. Scherer, and G. Palazzo. 2008. "Globalization, Transnational Corporations and the Future of Global Governance." In *Handbook of Research on Global Corporate Citizenship, Edward Elgar, Cheltenham*, 249–272.

[26] Stiglitz, J.E., and D. Rodrik. 2024. Rethinking Global Governance: Cooperation in a World of Power. *Research Paper. Cambridge, MA.*

[27] Dayen, D. 2015. "Bring Back Antitrust." *The American Prospect* 26, no. 4, pp. 46–53. Available at: http://prospect.org/article/bring-back-antitrust-0 (accessed December 02, 2019).

[28] Davis, G.F. 2015. *Capital Markets and Job Creation in the 21st Century.* Center for Effective Public Management, Brookings Institute, 1 September, 2016. Retrieved at https://www.brookings.edu/wp-content/uploads/2016/07/capital_markets.pdf.

[29] National Employment Law Project. 2012. Big Business, Corporate Profits, and the Minimum Wage, Data Brief.

[30] Browning, L., and D. Kocieniewski. 2016. "Pinning Down Apple's Alleged 0.005% Tax Rate is Nearly Impossible." *Bloomberg Technology (site).* https://www. bloomberg. com/news/articles/2016-09-01/pinning-down-apple-s-alleged-0-005-tax-ratemission-impossible.

[31] https://aflcio.org/paywatch?utm_source=chatgpt.com.

[32] Fed Rate Cuts should Boost Corporate America's Buyback Binge. https://www.ft.com/content/39c08b7d-e4f4-4141-a05a-f0299eef1466?utm_source=chatgpt.com.

[33] https://markets.businessinsider.com/news/stocks/meta-platforms-stock-market-outlook-mark-zuckerberg-buybacks-investing-analysis-2024-2?utm_source=chatgpt.com.

[34] Nallareddy, S., E. Rouen, and J.C.S. Serrato. 2022. "Do Corporate Tax Cuts Increase Income Inequality?." *Tax Policy and the Economy* 36, no. 1, pp. 35–91.

[35] Hacker, J.S., and P. Pierson. 2010. *Winner-Take-All Politics: How Washington Made the Rich Richer--and Turned Its Back on the Middle Class.* Simon and Schuster.

[36] Wilkinson, R.G., and K.E. Pickett. 2009. "Income Inequality and Social Dysfunction." *Annual Review of Sociology* 35 no. 1, pp. 493–511.

CHAPTER 9

The Global Health and Well-Being

The Importance of the Health Care Sector

The health care sector spans a wide array of interrelated industries—from pharmaceuticals and biotechnology to medical devices, health care services, residential care, and managed care. It is a cornerstone of modern economies. As of 2023, annual U.S. health care spending reached $4.9 trillion (around 17.6% of GDP), with per-person expenditure averaging $14,570 [1]. That figure places the United States well above other high-income economies, which average around 11.5 percent of GDP [2].

Historically, health care has been one of the fastest-growing components of GDP. In 2023, health care spending grew 7.5 percent, outpacing overall economic growth at 6.6 percent—the highest spike since the early 2000s, excluding the COVID-19 surge [3]. Spending is heavily concentrated in personal health care—84.4 percent of total expenditures—primarily covering hospital care, physician services, and prescription drugs [3].

Globally, the health care services market is on a steep upward trajectory. It is projected to grow from $8.78 trillion in 2024 to $9.25 trillion in 2025, then reach $11.22 trillion by 2029. Meanwhile, the overall global health care market—encompassing pharmaceuticals, biotech, medical devices, and services—is valued at over $21 trillion in 2023, with expectations to more than double to nearly $45 trillion by 2032 [4]. Additionally, health care facilities management—a critical but often overlooked subsector—is estimated at $326 billion in 2024, and forecasted to rise to $837 billion by 2034 [5].

This expansive economic footprint reflects more than market size—it underscores the health care system's central role in societal well-being.

Health expenditures per capita, U.S. dollars, 2022 and 2023 (current expenditures and PPP adjusted)

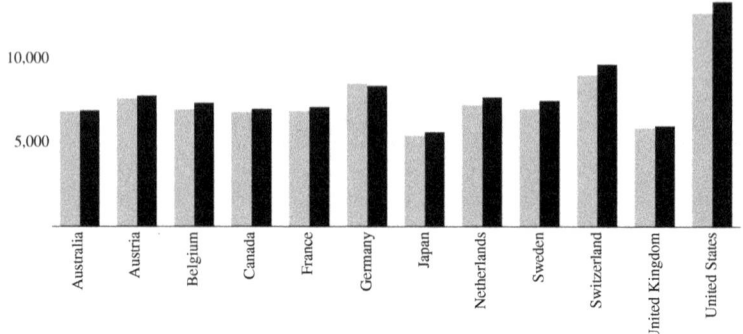

Notes: Data for 2023 from Australia, Belgium, Japan, the Netherlands, Switzerland, and United States are estimated.
Data for 2023 from Austria, Canada, France, Germany, Sweden and the United Kingdom are provisional. Data for 2022 for Australia, Canada and Japan are provisional.

Figure 9.1 Health expenditure per capita

Source: Health System Tracker [2].

Health expenditures per capita, U.S. dollars, 2023 (current prices and PPP adjusted)

United States	$13,432
Switzerland	$9,688
Germany	$8,441
Austria	$7,811
Netherlands	$7,737
Sweden	$7,522
Comparable Country Average	$7,393
Belgium	$7,380
France	$7,136
Canada	$7,013
Australia	$6,931
United Kingdom	$6,023
Japan	$5,640

Notes: Data from Australia, Belgium, Japan, the Netherlands, Switzerland, and United States are estimated. Data from Austria, Canada, France, Germany, Sweden and the United Kingdom are provisional.

Figure 9.2 Health expenditure per capita

Source: Health System Tracker [2].

Beyond treating illness, the sector supports employment: for instance, in the United States, it has driven roughly 40 percent of new private-sector jobs since early 2023, despite mixed health outcomes, including shorter average life expectancies and high chronic disease rates [6].

Looking forward, the sector faces transformation driven by several intersecting forces: an aging global population, technological innovation, rising chronic disease burdens, geopolitical shifts, and economic pressures. Digital health solutions are rapidly expanding—valued at $660 billion by 2025, up from $175 billion in 2019, and growing at nearly 25 percent annually [7]. Pharmaceutical innovation continues to offer cost-saving potential—such as obesity drugs like Ozempic, potentially reducing long-term health care spending by up to $250 billion annually [8].

Increasing Life Expectancy and Aging Populations

Global life expectancy has more than doubled over the past century, from approximately 32 years around 1900 to about 73.4 years in 2023 (70.8 for males, 76.0 for females) [9]. This improvement—driven by advances in sanitation, nutrition, health care, and education—varies significantly across regions. Between 2000 and 2019, average life expectancy rose from 66.8 to 73.1 years, while healthy life expectancy improved from 58.1 to 63.5 years [10, 11]. However, the COVID-19 pandemic reversed approximately a decade's worth of gains, with both metrics falling back to 2012 levels by 2021 [12]. However, projections suggest a continued upward trend if global health systems adapt accordingly, especially in the post-pandemic context.

Population aging is occurring at an unprecedented pace. In 2020, roughly one billion people were aged 60 or older; this figure is expected to more than double to about 2.1 billion by 2050 [12]. By then, 80 percent of older individuals will reside in low- and middle-income countries. Similarly, those aged 65 and above are projected to rise from 761 million in 2021 to 1.6 billion by 2050 [11]. The subset aged 80 and over is expected to triple to approximately 426 million [12].

In 2025, people aged 65+ already represent about 10 percent of the global population—a share set to climb to around 16 percent by 2050. By 2080, those aged 65 and older are projected to outnumber children under 18 [11].

Regional aging dynamics differ markedly. While developed countries remain the most aged, the most rapid growth in their elderly populations is happening in developing nations. Between 2010 and 2050, the 65+ population will increase by over 250 percent in developing countries, compared to 71 percent in developed ones [12]. In Asia—particularly China and India—aging trends are especially pronounced. For instance, in China, the 65+ population is projected to rise from 110 million in 2015 to 330 million by 2050; in India, the increase is from 60 million to over 227 million [12]. The United States is also aging dramatically: Americans aged 65 and older are projected to increase from 58 million in 2022 to 82 million by 2050, raising their share from 17 to 23 percent of the population [13]. Notably, the share of older Americans identifying as non-Hispanic white is expected to drop from 75 to 60 percent, reflecting growing diversity among elders [13].

These demographic shifts impose significant burdens on global systems. Health and social care infrastructures must expand to meet growing demands, particularly to manage noncommunicable diseases (NCDs) such as cardiovascular illnesses, cancers, diabetes, and dementia [10]. Economically, aging populations strain pension systems, health care financing, and labor markets—fewer working-age adults will have to support more retirees. The United States, for instance, faces persistent life expectancy gaps compared to peer countries, despite significantly higher health care spending [2].

In summary, the accelerating trend toward a globally aging population—coupled with rising longevity—is reshaping societal needs. Proactive policies are vital: expanding preventive care, adapting workplaces for older adults, ensuring sustainable pension and health care systems, and supporting healthy aging—particularly in low- and middle-income regions—are essential to a stable demographic and economic future.

The Rising Burden of Noncommunicable Diseases

As societies undergo economic development, they typically experience declining fertility and mortality rates alongside improvements in life expectancy. These demographic transitions are accompanied by an epidemiological shift—from infectious and parasitic diseases, which once dominated early 20th-century mortality patterns, to NCDs that predominantly affect adults and the elderly. While infectious diseases remain prevalent in many low-income countries due to poverty, poor sanitation,

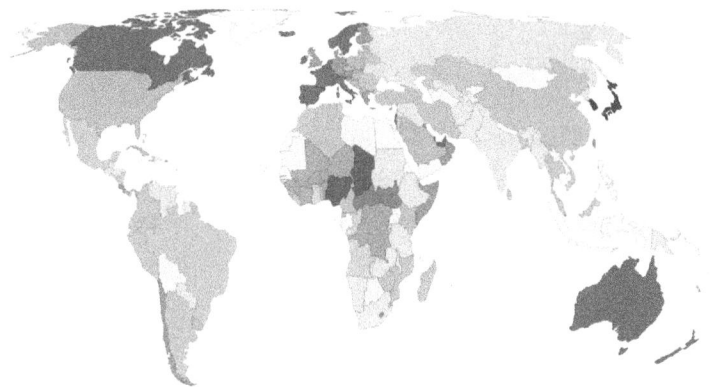

Figure 9.3 A world map of life expectancy at birth, 2023

Source: Based on the United Nations estimates (2023) [11].

and malnutrition, rising living standards are increasingly bringing NCDs to the forefront of global health concerns [14].

NCDs now represent a growing burden in both developed and developing countries. These diseases include cardiovascular conditions, cancers, chronic respiratory illnesses, diabetes, and mental disorders. The WHO projects that in the next 10 to 15 years, NCDs will surpass infectious diseases as the leading cause of death and disability in every region of the world. In 2008, NCDs accounted for 86 percent of deaths in high-income countries, 65 percent in middle-income countries, and 37 percent in low-income countries. By 2030, these figures are expected to rise to 75 percent and 50 percent for middle- and low-income countries, respectively, while deaths from infectious diseases will decline to 10 and 30 percent [14, 15].

The growing incidence of NCDs is attributed to multiple interrelated factors. These include rapid urbanization, population aging, sedentary lifestyles, poor dietary habits, widespread tobacco and alcohol use, and limited physical activity [15]. Additionally, exposure to environmental pollutants, air and water contamination, excessive consumption of processed foods high in sugar, salt, and saturated fats, and the psychosocial stress associated with modern life contribute significantly to this global health crisis [16]. Obesity, in particular, is a significant risk factor for many NCDs, including cardiovascular disease, stroke, type 2 diabetes, and several forms of cancer [17]. According to the National Health and Nutrition Examination Survey (NHANES), the prevalence of obesity among older adults in the United States stands at 34.6 percent [18].

Globally, NCDs are responsible for approximately 40 million deaths each year—accounting for nearly 70 percent of all deaths. Of these, cardiovascular diseases cause the highest number of deaths (17.7 million annually), followed by cancers (8.8 million), chronic respiratory diseases (3.9 million), and diabetes (1.6 million) (WHO, 2021). The economic consequences are profound. At the individual level, patients and their families often face impoverishment due to the long-term costs of care. An estimated 100 million people fall into poverty each year as a result of health expenditures linked to chronic conditions [18]. At the national level, productivity losses due to workforce reduction and disability further exacerbate economic strain. According to the World Economic Forum (2008), emerging economies such as Brazil, China, India, South Africa, and Russia lost over 20 million productive life years in 2000 due to cardiovascular disease alone. The cumulative economic losses from NCDs are projected to exceed $47 trillion over the next two decades, severely impeding global economic growth and development.

Mental health disorders, particularly dementia and Alzheimer's disease, are also rising rapidly and pose a unique challenge due to their chronic, degenerative nature and association with aging. Dementia is characterized by a decline in memory, cognitive function, and the ability to perform everyday tasks. However, it often remains underdiagnosed, especially in low-resource settings, leading to gaps in global data. According to the OECD, in 2000, dementia affected approximately 10 million people in member countries—7 percent of individuals aged 65 and older. Alzheimer's disease accounted for between 40 and 80 percent of these cases [14].

The global prevalence of dementia is estimated at 27 to 36 million people today, with numbers projected to rise to 115 million by 2050 (Alzheimer's Disease International, 2015). The risk increases sharply with age: only 3 percent of individuals aged 65–69 are affected, compared to 30 percent of those aged 85–89. Studies in France and Germany show that over half of women aged 90 and above suffer from some form of dementia [14].

The economic burden is immense. The World Alzheimer Report estimated the total global cost of dementia at over $600 billion in 2010 [14]. This figure is expected to rise exponentially as aging populations expand, especially in low- and middle-income countries that allocate less than 2 percent of their health budgets to mental health care [4]. Most individuals with dementia eventually lose independence and require full-time assistance, placing substantial physical, emotional, and financial strain on families and communities. The challenge is compounded by shrinking family sizes and fewer caregivers available to support the elderly.

To address this growing crisis, both national governments and international institutions must prioritize integrated health strategies that combine prevention, early diagnosis, community support, and long-term care solutions. Without decisive action, the dual burden of physical and mental NCDs will continue to erode global health, exacerbate inequality, and threaten sustainable development.

The Growing Risks of Pandemics

Despite remarkable progress in medicine and public health, communicable diseases continue to pose a serious global threat, particularly in low- and middle-income countries. Diseases such as malaria, tuberculosis, HIV/AIDS, bacterial diarrhea, and cholera still claim millions of lives each year. Poverty remains a key driver of these outbreaks, as poor living conditions, inadequate sanitation, and lack of access to clean water create fertile ground for the spread of infectious pathogens. According to a joint report by the WHO and UNICEF, one-third of the global population still lacks access to proper toilets [19]. In India alone, an estimated 564 million people practice open defecation, releasing over 65,000 tons of fecal matter into the environment daily.

Malnutrition, often linked to poverty, weakens the immune system and increases vulnerability to infections. Low levels of education and limited public health awareness further exacerbate these conditions. Cholera, for example, affects between 1.4 and 4.3 million people globally each year and causes approximately 143,000 deaths. The 2014 Ebola outbreak in West Africa resulted in more than 11,000 deaths. HIV/AIDS remains a significant health challenge, with 36 million people living with the disease worldwide—most of them in sub-Saharan Africa [20].

Moreover, the emergence of new communicable diseases has become increasingly frequent. Between 1940 and 2004, over 300 novel infectious diseases were identified. Many of these are linked to environmental degradation, deforestation, intensive livestock farming, and genetic mutations in pathogens. Recent examples include SARS (2003), avian influenza (2006–2010), H1N1 influenza (2009), Ebola (2014), and MERS (2015).

The COVID-19 pandemic, which began in late 2019, dramatically underscored the global threat posed by infectious diseases. Within weeks of its initial outbreak in Wuhan, China, COVID-19 spread across continents, infecting hundreds of millions and claiming over 6.9 million lives by 2024. Unlike previous outbreaks, COVID-19 disrupted not only health systems but also economies, education, transportation, and global supply chains. Entire countries were placed under lockdown, borders were sealed, and major cities came to a halt. The pandemic exposed systemic weaknesses in public health infrastructure, emergency preparedness, and global coordination, even in high-income nations.

Several factors have intensified the threat of pandemics in recent decades. Rapid industrialization, population growth, dense urban settlements, high concentrations of livestock, and environmental degradation create optimal conditions for zoonotic spillover and pathogen evolution. Many developing countries lack basic health care infrastructure and sanitation, making containment difficult once an outbreak begins. Globalization further compounds the risk: modern transportation networks enable pathogens to travel across continents in mere hours. For example, during the 2003 SARS epidemic, international air travel was a key vector for global spread. Today, with vastly increased travel volumes, a virulent outbreak could reach every major city within 60 days and potentially cause tens of millions of deaths [20].

Pandemics also carry far-reaching socioeconomic consequences. Governments often respond with emergency measures—closing schools, workplaces, and markets; restricting movement; and reallocating public resources to the health sector. These actions, while necessary, can trigger economic recessions, unemployment, supply chain disruptions, and inflation. The psychological impact, including widespread fear, anxiety, and mistrust, can erode public confidence in institutions. COVID-19 illustrated how even unaffected regions can experience economic hardship due to global interconnectedness.

Looking forward, the risk of future pandemics remains high. Lessons from COVID-19 and earlier outbreaks highlight the urgent need for investment in disease surveillance, early warning systems, health care infrastructure, and coordinated global response mechanisms. Without significant reforms and international cooperation, the world will continue to face the devastating human, economic, and political consequences of emerging infectious diseases.

The Upsurge in Medication Expenditure

Global spending on medicines has been rising steadily and continues to grow at a significant pace. According to the IQVIA Institute for Human Data Science (2023), worldwide medicine expenditures are projected to exceed $1.9 trillion by 2027, mainly driven by oncology treatments, immunology drugs, diabetes care, and the expansion of specialty medicines. The global pharmaceutical market is expanding at an average annual rate of 3–6 percent, with emerging markets outpacing developed economies in terms of growth [21].

The United States remains the largest pharmaceutical market, accounting for nearly 40 percent of global pharmaceutical sales. U.S. medicine spending is expected to grow by 4–7 percent annually over the next five years due to the increased use of high-cost specialty drugs, biologics, and new therapies. China continues to hold the position of the second-largest pharmaceutical market, while other emerging economies such as Brazil, India, Mexico, and Turkey are experiencing faster growth compared to developed countries [21].

Developed economies—including the United States, Japan, Germany, the United Kingdom, Italy, France, Spain, Canada, South Korea, and Australia—remain the top markets in terms of overall expenditure. However, their growth rates are slowing relative to developing countries, where generic and biosimilar products dominate the market. In contrast, developed economies spend disproportionately on branded and patented medications.

Oncology remains the primary driver of pharmaceutical spending, with global cancer drug expenditures surpassing $196 billion in 2022, and forecasted to exceed $375 billion by 2027 [21]. Diabetes treatments, along with biologics for autoimmune conditions, are also contributing significantly to overall growth. Spending on biologics for autoimmune diseases is expected to continue rising sharply, with therapies such as monoclonal antibodies and novel immunotherapies leading the trend.

In the United States, medication prices are already among the highest in the world and continue to rise. A study found that retail prices for 113 chronic-use brand-name drugs increased by 188.7 percent between 2006 and 2015. Prescription drug costs now constitute nearly 20 percent of total health care expenditures, and patients—particularly older adults—are disproportionately burdened by these costs. By 2023, the average annual out-of-pocket cost for seniors requiring multiple medications exceeded $30,000, reflecting a continued upward trajectory in drug prices [22].

Specialty drugs, which are used for the treatment of complex or chronic conditions such as cancer, rheumatoid arthritis, multiple sclerosis, and rare genetic disorders, are a key factor driving U.S. drug spending. These drugs, often delivered via injectables or requiring special storage and handling, accounted for nearly 50 percent of total drug expenditures in the United States in 2022 [23]. Between 2014 and 2022, spending on specialty medicines grew at a rate nearly three times higher than that of traditional medicines.

The rapid growth of specialty drugs has also fueled the expansion of specialty pharmacies, which focus on managing the distribution, handling, and patient support services required for these complex therapies. According to industry reports, the specialty pharmacy segment is projected to grow by 8–10 percent annually, reflecting the strong pipeline of high-cost, innovative therapies entering the market.

The continued rise in global and U.S. medication expenditures poses significant challenges for health care systems, insurers, employers, and patients. Without systemic reforms in drug pricing, regulation, and innovation incentives, the cost of pharmaceuticals is likely to remain one of the most pressing issues in global health care over the coming decade.

The Rising Cost of Care and the Global Shortage of Health Care Workers

Over the coming decades, rising life expectancy and rapidly aging populations are expected to place unprecedented strain on health care systems worldwide. As demand for health services increases, both patients and governments will be forced to spend significantly more to sustain acceptable levels of care. According to the Economist Intelligence Unit and Deloitte (2023), global health care spending is projected to grow at an average annual rate of 5.3 percent, reaching over $10 trillion by 2030 [24].

This surge in expenditure presents a growing challenge, particularly in societies where the proportion of the economically active population is shrinking. For instance, the EU is projected to lose 48 million working-age individuals (aged 15–64) by 2050, which will undermine the tax base and strain public health care financing [25]. Simultaneously, health care costs are being driven upward by multiple factors: increased utilization of services, overprescription of medications, and the development of new technologies and treatments. While innovations enhance health outcomes, they also come with high price tags. In some cases, pharmaceutical companies have dramatically raised prices by 5,000 to 6,000 percent in just a few years. A notorious example occurred in 2015 when Turing Pharmaceuticals acquired the life-saving antiparasitic drug *Daraprim* and increased its price overnight from $13.50 to $750 per pill [26].

The growing number of individuals living with multiple chronic conditions—such as diabetes, cardiovascular disease, and dementia—further compounds the challenge. These patients typically require complex, long-term, and expensive care. As a result, health care systems, regardless of their design, are encountering spending increasingly unsustainable trajectories. In high-income countries, access to acute and institutional long-term care is relatively standard, but the growing elderly population is increasing per capita health care utilization. In contrast, many developing countries are still in the process of building basic health care infrastructure and estimating disease prevalence, placing them at a significant disadvantage.

Alongside rising costs, health care systems are also facing a severe and growing shortage of health professionals. According to the WHO, in 2013, 118 out of 186 countries were already experiencing a shortfall of 7.2 million skilled health workers. This deficit is projected to reach nearly 13 million by 2035 [27]. Several factors, including the retirement of aging workers, insufficient training pipelines, low wages, burnout, and migration to higher-paying sectors drive the health care labor crisis. To bridge workforce gaps, many high-income countries have become heavily reliant on foreign-trained medical professionals. For example, 35 percent of physicians in England are foreign nationals, while the share reaches up to 80 percent in Oman, the UAE, and Saudi Arabia [22]. This trend exacerbates the brain drain from lower-income nations, which are often left with dangerously depleted health workforces.

Compounding the crisis is the erosion of traditional family structures, particularly in Western societies. Over the last four decades, rising rates of divorce, remarriage, single parenthood, and same-sex partnerships have redefined the nuclear family. These changes have resulted in fewer siblings, smaller extended families, and reduced familial caregiving capacity for elderly individuals. In the United States, for example, the percentage of divorced individuals stands at 9 percent for those aged 65 and older, 17 percent for those ages 55–64, and 18 percent for those aged 45–54 [14]. As a result, future generations of older adults will have fewer family members to rely on for informal care.

This lack of familial support disproportionately affects women. Unmarried women are significantly less likely than unmarried men to accumulate sufficient savings and pension assets for later life, leaving them more vulnerable to financial insecurity and unmet care needs. As demographic and social transformations converge with rising health care costs and workforce shortages, a comprehensive and forward-looking policy response will be essential to sustain equitable and efficient health care systems across the globe.

Toward the Globalization of the Health Care Sector

While globalization has reshaped industries such as manufacturing, finance, insurance, investment, and information technology, the health care sector has remained comparatively localized—mainly due to regulatory, linguistic, cultural, and legal constraints. However, this pattern is beginning to change. Rising health care costs and increasing demand for high-quality services are compelling businesses, consumers, and policymakers to seek efficiencies through global integration. As no single country possesses all the necessary health care resources—such as trained personnel, pharmaceuticals, advanced technologies, or infrastructure—cross-border collaboration is becoming increasingly essential.

Over the past three decades, national health systems have explored global solutions to local challenges, particularly through the exchange of skilled health care workers. For example, the United States and the United Kingdom have long relied on migrant nurses from countries such as the Philippines, South Africa, and the Caribbean. Filipino nurses, in particular, have benefited from significant wage differentials, earning up to nine times more in the United Kingdom than at home [28, 29]. Similarly, the U.S. health care system has become increasingly reliant on foreign-trained medical professionals. As of 2022, nearly 25 percent of practicing physicians in the United States were educated abroad, predominantly from countries like India, Pakistan, the Philippines, and other English-speaking nations [30].

This globalization of human capital is not limited to Anglo-American countries. More than 50 countries, including Australia, Brazil, Sweden, Malaysia, and the UAE, now integrate foreign health care professionals into their national systems [28]. This global workforce migration helps address labor shortages in high-income countries while creating remittance-based economic support in the sending countries.

Globalization is also transforming the pharmaceutical and biotechnology industries. Multinational pharmaceutical companies now conduct R&D operations across borders, utilizing global supply chains and pursuing clinical trials in lower-cost countries such as India, Brazil, and Eastern Europe. Clinical trials conducted in emerging markets offer reduced costs and faster patient recruitment, accelerating drug development timelines.

In addition, many American hospitals and diagnostic centers outsource radiology and medical imaging services to providers in countries such as India, Israel, Australia, Switzerland, and Lebanon, allowing for overnight turnaround of CT scans, MRIs, and X-rays. Advances in telemedicine,

AI-assisted diagnostics, and cloud-based health information systems are further blurring national boundaries in health care delivery.

Another key dimension of health care globalization involves the standardization of medical practices and regulatory frameworks. As pharmaceutical companies expand globally, there is growing momentum toward harmonizing drug approval procedures, safety protocols, and quality standards. This need for alignment is especially urgent in countries with universal health care systems, where taxpayers demand transparency, efficiency, and equitable outcomes. Cross-border benchmarking, shared data platforms, and international collaboration are becoming increasingly common among health care regulators and hospital systems.

Despite these advances, the globalization of health care also brings risks. Critics warn of rising health care costs, uneven service quality, and inequities in access—especially in underresourced regions. There are concerns that global consolidation in the pharmaceutical and hospital industries may prioritize profits over patient outcomes, creating disparities in affordability and treatment availability. Moreover, the outflow of health care professionals from low-income to high-income countries can exacerbate shortages in the countries of origin, undermining local health care delivery.

Nevertheless, the globalization of health care presents enormous opportunities for innovation, efficiency, and improved outcomes—particularly if managed through thoughtful regulation and international cooperation. As global health crises like COVID-19 have demonstrated, disease knows no borders, and the future of health care will increasingly depend on the ability of nations to collaborate, coordinate, and adapt in a globally interconnected system.

The Digitization of Health Care

Despite significant advances in biomedical science and medical technologies, the health care sector has lagged behind other industries in adopting digital solutions. However, this is changing rapidly. The digitization of health care is expected to fundamentally transform the sector over the next two decades by enhancing efficiency, improving outcomes, and expanding access—especially in the face of rising costs, aging populations, and chronic disease burdens.

However, the transition is not without obstacles. Regulatory constraints, data privacy concerns, fragmented health systems, and institutional resistance continue to hinder the widespread adoption of digital technologies. For example, as recently as 2022, surveys indicated that nearly two-thirds of U.S. physicians were reluctant to grant patients full access to their own health records, despite growing consumer demand for transparency and control over personal health data [31]. Nonetheless, the financial and logistical pressures on health care systems are forcing innovation, and digitization is increasingly viewed as essential for sustainability.

Digital transformation in health care involves two primary disruptions: a shift in the location of care and a shift in the type of care delivered. The first refers to the migration of care from hospitals to homes and community settings, made possible by telemedicine, remote monitoring, and home-based diagnostic tools. The second involves a pivot from reactive treatment toward preventive and chronic disease management, empowering patients to actively monitor and manage their health with minimal reliance on in-person visits.

With the rise of wearable devices, intelligent diagnostics, and mobile health (mHealth) platforms, patients can now track vital signs, access personalized care plans, and receive medical consultations remotely. This shift enhances convenience, expands access to underserved regions, and significantly reduces health care costs. Importantly, digital solutions are data-driven, improving diagnostic precision, treatment adherence, and clinical decision making.

Consumer-centric models are emerging, where individuals assume greater responsibility for their health through digital tools, reducing dependency on clinicians. Health kiosks, AI-powered apps, and digital assistants allow users to consult with health care providers, schedule virtual appointments, and review medical records from their smartphones or tablets. Companies like HealthTap and Teladoc Health exemplify this trend. HealthTap has developed an expansive virtual network of over 100,000 physicians and more than 10 million users, enabling patients to connect with doctors via apps on smartphones and tablets. Teladoc offers remote, on-demand medical care through phone, video, and online platforms and has become a leader in telehealth services, particularly during the COVID-19 pandemic [32].

Digitization is also transforming care delivery through robotic surgery, 3D medical printing, precision medicine, and AI diagnostics. These technologies allow for tailored treatment plans, minimally invasive procedures, and reduced hospitalization times. The integration of electronic health records (EHRs), cloud-based data sharing, and interoperable platforms is improving coordination between providers and reducing administrative overhead.

The global digital health market has expanded rapidly. According to recent estimates, it reached $330 billion in 2022 and is projected to surpass $660 billion by 2027, driven by growth in telemedicine, mobile health, electronic patient records, wearables, and AI-assisted technologies [33]. Telemedicine, in particular, saw exponential growth during the COVID-19 pandemic, with usage increasing by over 400 percent in some regions between 2020 and 2021. As of 2023, more than 80 percent of U.S. states require insurers to reimburse virtual care services on par with in-person consultations.

Ultimately, digitization is shifting the health care system toward value-based care, where patient outcomes, efficiency, and satisfaction are prioritized over volume. By bridging the gap between the digital and physical worlds, digital health tools are enabling more personalized, accessible, and sustainable care systems. However, realizing the full potential of digital health will require robust data governance, equity in access, and collaboration among governments, providers, and technology developers.

Toward a Personalized, Precise, and Robotic Medicine

Traditional medical treatments have been mainly designed for the "average patient," assuming similar responses across the population. However, individuals often respond very differently to the same treatment. Research shows that 30–40 percent of patients receive medications that are either ineffective or cause adverse side effects, underscoring the urgent need for more individualized approaches to care.

Advances in genomic sequencing, cloud computing, big data analytics, and AI are accelerating the shift toward precision medicine—an emerging model of care that customizes treatments based on an individual's genetic makeup, environment, and lifestyle. This approach aims to improve the accuracy of disease prevention, diagnosis, and treatment by tailoring interventions to patient-specific variables. In oncology, for instance, genomic profiling is now commonly used to develop targeted therapies that attack cancer cells based on unique genetic mutations [34].

With ongoing improvements in data science and bioinformatics, it is estimated that over 60 percent of patients could benefit from genomic-guided health care within the next decade. Companies such as Illumina, Foundation Medicine, and 23andMe have experienced significant growth by offering genomic testing and personalized diagnostics, helping to usher in a new era of preventive, predictive, and participatory medicine.

In parallel, robotic technologies are revolutionizing surgery and health care delivery. Robot-assisted surgery is increasingly being adopted worldwide due to its benefits in enabling minimally invasive procedures, reducing recovery time, lowering infection risks, and improving surgical precision. These systems allow surgeons to operate robotic arms via a computer console, enhancing dexterity and control during delicate procedures. In 2023, the global medical robotics market surpassed $16 billion and is projected to reach $44 billion by 2030, driven by aging populations, chronic disease management, and the demand for surgical accuracy [35].

The Da Vinci Surgical System, a leading robotic platform, was used in more than 1.8 million surgeries globally in 2022, ranging from urology and gynecology to general surgery [34]. Beyond surgery, robotics is being deployed for diagnostics, pharmacy automation, elder care, and hospital logistics. For example, Baidu Health has introduced an AI-powered application using natural language processing and voice recognition to suggest diagnoses based on user-entered symptoms, directing patients to appropriate health care providers.

Another disruptive force in personalized medicine is 3D printing (also known as additive manufacturing). This technology allows for the production of customized implants, prosthetics, dental devices, surgical tools, and even pharmaceuticals, tailored to individual patient needs. The global health care 3D printing market was valued at $2.5 billion in 2022 and is projected to exceed $10 billion by 2030, with applications expanding rapidly in orthopedics, craniofacial reconstruction, bioprinting, and drug formulation [36].

3D printing enables faster, decentralized production—often within hospitals—reducing supply chain delays and costs. For example, hospitals can now print patient-specific surgical guides or implants on-site, improving surgical outcomes and efficiency. Researchers are also exploring bioprinting, where living cells are layered to form tissues and, eventually, organs for transplantation.

The convergence of genomics, robotics, AI, and 3D printing is paving the way toward a health care paradigm that is precise, efficient, and patient-centered. This next frontier of medicine promises not only improved clinical outcomes but also enhanced affordability, especially as economies of scale and digital infrastructure evolve. However, achieving its full potential will require robust data privacy safeguards, updated regulatory frameworks, and equitable access to these innovations across diverse populations.

References

[1] World Economic Forum. 2024. Is This How Healthcare will be Optimized in the Future? https://www.weforum.org/stories/2024/12/healthcare-hospital-of-the-future/?utm_source=chatgpt.com.

[2] Health System Tracker. 2025. How Does Health Spending in the US Compare to Other Countries?

[3] Hardiman, A. 2025. Policy Research Perspectives.

[4] Global News Wire. 2025. https://www.globenewswire.com/news-release/2024/08/01/2923001/0/en/Healthcare-Market-Size-Worth-US-44-760-73-Billion-By-2032-Continuous-Advancements-in-Biotechnology-Pharmaceuticals-Propels-Growth-Research-by-SNS-Insider.html?

[5] Precedence Research. https://www.precedenceresearch.com/healthcare-facilities-management-market?

[6] Financial Times. 2024, June 11. "America: A Healthy or Healthcare Economy? The Sickness at the Heart of US GDP." *Financial Times*. https://www.ft.com/content/4a2cfd3b-f692-49df-9857-771e2e39d85b.

[7] Sen, M. 2024, December 19. "Is This How Healthcare will be Optimized in the Future?" *World Economic Forum*. https://www.weforum.org/stories/2024/12/healthcare-hospital-of-the-future/.

[8] Reuters. 2024, July 17. "Ozempic May Gift US a $3 trln Benefit." *Reuters Breakingviews*. Retrieved from https://www.reuters.com/breakingviews/ozempic-may-gift-us-3-trln-benefit-2024-07-16/.

[9] World Population Review. n.d. Life Expectancy by Country. Retrieved [August 17, 2025], from https://worldpopulationreview.com/country-rankings/life-expectancy-by-country

[10] World Health Organization. n.d. "GHE: Life Expectancy and Healthy Life Expectancy." *Global Health Observatory*. Retrieved August 17, 2025, from https://www.who.int/data/gho/data/themes/mortality-and-global-health-estimates/ghe-life-expectancy-and-healthy-life-expectancy?

[11] World Population Prospects. 2024. (XLSX). United Nations Department of Economic and Social Affairs. July 27, 2024.

[12] World Health Organization. 2025. "GHE: Life Expectancy and Healthy Life Expectancy." *Global Health Observatory* data repository. Retrieved August 18, 2025, from https://www.who.int/data/gho/data/themes/mortality-and-global-health-estimates/ghe-life-expectancy-and-healthy-life-expectancy.

[13] Mather, M., and Scommegna, P. 2024, January 9. "Fact Sheet: Aging in the United States." *Population Reference Bureau*. Retrieved August 18, 2025, from https://www.prb.org/resources/fact-sheet-aging-in-the-united-states/?utm_source=chatgpt.com.

[14] World Health Organization. 2011. *Global Health and Aging*. Geneva: World Health Organization.

[15] World Health Organization. 2021. "WHO Results Report 2020–2021." Retrieved August 18, 2025, from https://www.who.int/about/accountability/results/who-results-report-2020-2021.

[16] Scrutton, J., G. Holley-Moore, and S.M. Bamford. 2015. *Creating a Sustainable 21st Century Healthcare System*. International Longevity Centre–UK (ILC-UK).

[17] Bloom, D.E., and R. McKinnon. 2010. *Introduction: Social Security and the Challenge of Demographic Change (No. 6110)*. Program on the Global Demography of Aging.

[18] Beglaryan, M., V. Petrosyan, and E. Bunker. 2017. "Development of a Tripolar Model of Technology Acceptance: Hospital-Based Physicians' Perspective on EHR." *International Journal of Medical Informatics*, 102, pp. 50–61.

[19] The Guardian. 2015. "Billions have no Access to Toilets, says World Health Organisation Report." https://theguardian.com/society/2015/jul/01/billions-have-no-access-to-toilets-says-world-health-organisation-report.

[20] Dobriansky, P.J., R.M. Suzman, and R.J. Hodes. 2007. *Why Population Aging Matters: A Global Perspective*. National Institute on Aging, National Institutes of Health, US Department of Health and Human Services, US Department of State.

[21] IQVIA Institute for Human Data Science. 2023, January 18. "The Global Use of Medicines 2023: Outlook to 2027." *IQVIA*. Retrieved August 18, 2025, from https://www.iqvia.com/insights/the-iqvia-institute/reports-and-publications/reports/the-global-use-of-medicines-2023.

[22] Schondelmeyer, S.W., and L. Purvis. 2016. Trends in Retail Prices of Brand Name Prescription Drugs Widely Used by Older Americans, 2006 to 2015.

[23] https://phrma.org/resources/.

[24] The Economist Intelligence Unit. 2022. "Healthcare Outlook 2023: The Aftermath of the Pandemic [PDF]." Retrieved August 18, 2025, from https://www.eiu.com/n/wp-content/uploads/2022/10/Healthcare-outlook-2023.pdf.

[25] Schwab, K., and M. Porter. 2008. *The Global Competitiveness Report 2008–2009*. World Economic Forum.

[26] Los Angeles Times. December 21, 2016. "How 4 Drug Companies Rapidly Raised Prices on Life-Saving Drugs." http://latimes.com/business/la-fi-senate-drug-price-study-20161221-story.html

[27] Healthcare, U. 2012. *Personalized Medicine: Trends and Prospects for the New Science of Genetic Testing and Molecular Diagnostics*. United Healthcare Center for Health Reform and Modernization: Minnetonka, Minnesota.

[28] Time.com. 2017. http://time.com/4658651/medical-school-foreign-doctorsstudy.

[29] IFC Global Conference. February 16–18, 2005. *Investing in Private Healthcare in Emerging Markets Conference*. International Finance Corporation (IFC): Washington, DC.

[30] Munro, D. June 08, 2015. "New Poll Shows Two-Thirds of Doctors Reluctant to Share Health Data with Patients." Forbes. http://forbes.com/sites/danmunro/2015/06/08/two%E2%80%92thirds-of-doctors-arereluctant-to-sharehealth-data-with-patients.

[31] Lapowsky, I. July 30, 2014. "HealthTap's Video Chatting Doctors Want to End Your WebMD Meltdowns." Wired. http://wired.com/2014/07/healthtap-prime/.

[32] Foundation Medicine. 2015. "Our Vision." http://foundationmedicine.com/.

[33] https://statista.com/statistics/225123/chinas-share-of-the-global-carmarket/.

[34] Global Medical Robotics Market Outlook. 2018. "PRNewswire." http://prnewswire.com/newsreleases/global-medical-robotics-marketoutlook-2018-300077013.html

[35] UnitedHealth Center for Health Reform & Modernization. 2012. "Personalized Medicine: Trends and Prospects for the New Science of Genetic Testing and Molecular Diagnostics." Working Paper 7, http://unitedhealthgroup.com/~/media/UHG/PDF/2012/UNH-Working-Paper-7.ashx.

[36] https://www.marketresearch.com/MarketsandMarkets-v3719/.

CHAPTER 10

Environmental Degradation

Environmental Degradation:
Its Rise and Defining Features

Environmental degradation is one of the most pressing global challenges of the 21st century. It refers to the decline in the environment's ability to meet ecological and social needs, encompassing a broad range of harmful changes to natural systems caused by both human activities and natural processes [1, 2]. While natural events such as droughts and volcanic eruptions can contribute, the primary drivers today are anthropogenic—particularly those associated with industrialization, urbanization, and resource-intensive economic growth.

The environment consists of abiotic components—air, water, and soil—and biotic elements such as plants, animals, and microorganisms [3]. Together, these components provide essential life-support functions: supplying clean air, water, and food; absorbing and processing waste; and sustaining habitats for diverse species. When these functions are compromised, environmental degradation occurs. The extent of this damage is often measured using indicators such as the ecological footprint, which assesses the degree to which human activity exceeds the Earth's regenerative capacity [4].

Environmental degradation manifests in multiple, interconnected forms. Key examples include climate change, global warming, greenhouse gas (GHG) emissions, air and water pollution, deforestation, desertification, biodiversity loss, overpopulation, and the overexploitation of natural resources. These processes not only disrupt ecosystems but also threaten human health and livelihoods. The impacts are especially severe in developing countries, where weaker environmental regulations and less robust health care systems contribute to environmental health risks estimated to be 15 times higher than in developed nations.

Over the past two decades, the growing urgency of these threats has drawn sustained attention from governments, international organizations, businesses, and academia. The Paris Agreement (2015) represents a significant milestone in global climate governance, setting targets for emissions reduction and promoting sustainable development. Many national governments have since adopted stricter environmental regulations and offered incentives for renewable energy adoption. Political movements, such as the Green Party, have been instrumental in mainstreaming environmental issues within political agendas.

The private sector has also responded by integrating environmental concerns into CSR strategies, recognizing that ecological decline poses material business risks [5]. At the same time, grassroots initiatives—particularly youth-led movements such as Fridays for Future—have amplified public pressure on both corporations and governments to take more decisive, science-based action.

Air Pollution

Air pollution refers to the presence of solid, liquid, or gaseous substances—such as smoke, nanoparticles, and radioactive materials—in the atmosphere at concentrations harmful to humans and other living organisms. Significant sources of air pollution include energy production, fossil fuel combustion, and transportation.

Particulate pollutants, which range from 0.001 to 500 micrometers (μm) in diameter, are primarily emitted by vehicles, power plants, construction activities, oil refineries, and industrial operations. Thermal power plants and coal-burning facilities release significant quantities of fly ash, which can cause heavy metal contamination. Lead particles, produced in significant amounts by vehicle exhaust, can remain suspended in the air for extended periods. Other metals—such as oxides of iron, aluminum, manganese, magnesium, and zinc—are discharged through mining, industrial, and metallurgical processes.

Gaseous pollutants encompass a broad range of chemicals, including carbon monoxide, nitrogen oxides, and sulfur dioxide. Burning one gallon of gasoline in a vehicle emits approximately 25 pounds of carbon dioxide (CO_2), along with other harmful substances such as carbon monoxide, sulfur dioxide, and nitrogen dioxide [6]. The rapid growth in vehicle ownership in emerging economies such as China and India has accelerated urban air pollution [7].

In addition to outdoor air pollution, indoor pollution remains a significant environmental health hazard in developing countries. The use of biomass-based cooking and heating stoves is a leading cause of respiratory diseases in these regions [8].

Air pollution poses severe risks to human health, contributing to respiratory infections, cardiovascular disease, and lung cancer. It also causes physiological, biochemical, and developmental harm to animals and plants. According to the WHO, global outdoor air pollution levels rose by 8 percent between 2008 and 2013, and more than 90 percent of the world's population is exposed to pollutant concentrations exceeding safe limits [9]. Air pollution is responsible for approximately 18,000 deaths per day—or 6.5 million deaths annually—making it the fourth-largest threat to human health worldwide [10].

Greenhouse Gas Emissions

GHG emissions refer to gases that trap heat in the Earth's atmosphere, thereby contributing to global warming. These include CO_2, methane (CH_4), nitrous oxide (N_2O), and various fluorinated gases [11]. The primary source of CO_2 is the combustion of fossil fuels, though other human activities—such as deforestation, agriculture, and waste management—also play significant roles in GHG emissions [12].

Different economic sectors contribute to GHG emissions to varying degrees: electricity and heat production account for approximately 25 percent, industry for 21 percent, agriculture and forestry for 24 percent, transportation for 14 percent, and building construction for 6 percent [13].

Global carbon emissions from fossil fuels have risen sharply over the past century, with the rate of increase accelerating particularly since the 1970s. Over the last three decades, GHG emissions have grown steadily as more developing countries have industrialized. For example, global GHG emissions from human activities in 2010 reached 46 billion metric tons—representing a 35 percent increase compared to 1990 levels [14] (Figures 10.1 and 10.2).

Annual greenhouse gas emissions by world region, 1850 to 2023

Greenhouse gas emissions[1] include carbon dioxide, methane and nitrous oxide from all sources, including land-use change. They are measured in tonnes of carbon dioxide-equivalents[2] over a 100-year timescale.

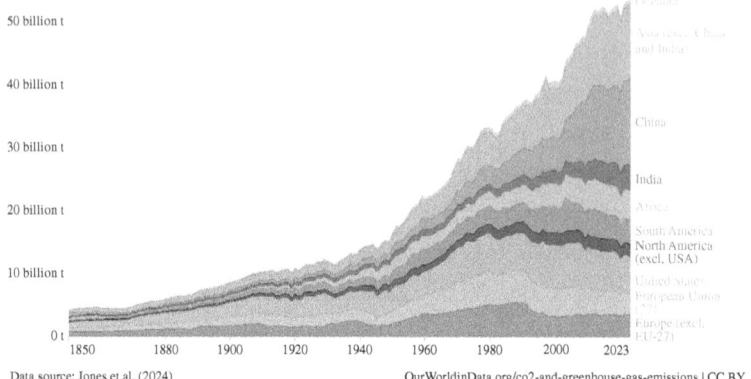

Data source: Jones et al. (2024)   OurWorldinData.org/co2-and-greenhouse-gas-emissions | CC BY

Figure 10.1 The growth of greenhouse gas emissions

Source: [16].

Greenhouse gas emissions, 2023

Greenhouse gas emissions[1] include carbon dioxide, methane and nitrous oxide from all sources, including land-use change. They are measured in tonnes of carbon dioxide-equivalents[2] over a 100-year timescale.

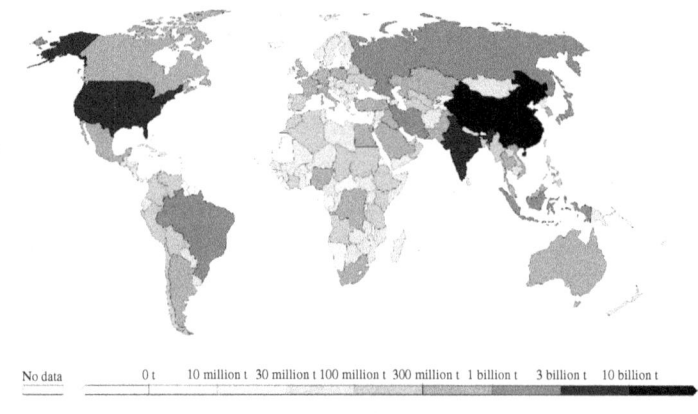

Data source: Jones et al. (2024)   OurWorldinData.org/co2-and-greenhouse-gas-emissions | CC BY
Note: Land-use change emissions can be negative.

Figure 10.2 Greenhouse gas emissions by country

Source: [17].

Future projections indicate continued growth. According to the OECD, global GHG emissions are expected to increase by about 37 percent between now and 2030, and by 52 percent between now and

2050 [15]. Emissions growth is projected to be significantly higher in developing nations than in wealthier, industrialized countries. In 2008, the largest CO_2 emitters were China, the United States, the EU, India, the Russian Federation, Japan, and Canada [14].

Global Warming

Global warming, closely linked to elevated levels of GHG emissions, is a central driver of climate change. It is now widely accepted in the scientific community that climate change is predominantly an anthropogenic phenomenon [18]. The acceleration of climate warming observed during the 20th century is unprecedented. Across nearly all continents, maximum temperatures, the number of hot days, and heat indices have increased markedly in the second half of the century [19].

Over the past century, the global average temperature has risen by approximately 0.7°C (1.3°F). Each successive decade—the 1980s, 1990s, and 2000s—has been warmer than the previous one. According to the National Oceanic and Atmospheric Administration, 2014 was the warmest year on record since 1880 [20]. The pace of warming continues to accelerate, with Arctic regions experiencing temperature increases faster than the global average. This rapid warming has contributed to significant ice melt, leading to a sea-level rise of about two millimeters per year [21]. Projections indicate that the Earth's average surface temperature could increase by between 1.4°C and 5.8°C by 2100 [22]. Importantly, these warming trends are expected to persist for decades, even if GHG emissions were halted immediately.

Rising global temperatures are already driving widespread changes in physical and biological systems. These include glacier retreat, altered rainfall patterns, shifts in growing seasons, earlier flowering of plants, earlier insect emergence, and changes in the geographic distribution of plant and animal species in response to shifting climatic conditions. Further temperature increases could severely disrupt the equilibrium of global ecosystems, causing irreversible and unpredictable transformations [23]. Potential climate-induced impacts include more frequent and intense heatwaves, flash floods, tropical storms, droughts, and other extreme weather events, as well as the spread of infectious diseases, scarcity of renewable resources, and accelerated sea-level rise. Additionally, global warming threatens to diminish the availability of fresh water and fertile soil, thereby reducing agricultural productivity and exacerbating food insecurity worldwide.

Ozone Depletion

The ozone layer, located in the Earth's stratosphere, plays a critical role in protecting the planet's surface from excessive ultraviolet (UV) radiation emitted by the sun. Exposure to high levels of UV radiation can be harmful to human health, ecosystems, and the environment. However, certain human-made chemicals—particularly chlorofluorocarbons (CFCs), which are used in refrigeration, air conditioning, fire extinguishers, cleaning solvents, and aerosol products—have been found to damage the ozone layer [24].

Over recent decades, the ozone layer has thinned significantly, reducing its ability to block harmful UV radiation. This depletion is most pronounced over the polar regions, with substantial ozone loss recorded over both the Arctic and Antarctic [25].

The consequences of ozone layer depletion are wide-ranging. For humans, increased UV exposure is associated with higher incidences of skin cancer, vision problems such as cataracts, and a weakened immune system. Beyond human health, ozone depletion contributes to climate change, degrades terrestrial and aquatic ecosystems, and reduces overall air quality [26].

Water Pollution

Water pollution is among the most severe environmental challenges, resulting from both human activities and natural processes. It affects diverse water bodies, including rivers, lakes, seas, oceans, estuaries, and groundwater sources. Major pollutants include nutrients, sediments, elevated temperatures, heavy metals, nonmetallic toxins, pesticides, and pathogenic microorganisms.

Human-driven sources are particularly significant. Agricultural and industrial runoff—laden with fertilizers, pesticides, toxic chemicals, and human and animal waste—continuously contaminates water resources.

Many industries, including power plants and nuclear reactors, use large volumes of water for cooling. When discharged back into rivers or lakes at elevated temperatures, this "thermal pollution" can disrupt aquatic ecosystems [27]. Another major contributor is eutrophication, the nutrient enrichment of water from domestic waste, agricultural runoff, and land drainage. This process can lead to sudden and massive fish kills, degrade water quality, and render it unsafe for human consumption [28].

The scale of the problem is immense. Each day, approximately 2 million tons of industrial, agricultural, and residential waste enter the world's water bodies [9]. In developing countries, an estimated 70 percent of industrial wastewater is discharged directly into natural waters without treatment [29]. Natural sources of water pollution include soil erosion, mineral leaching from rocks, and the decomposition of organic matter.

Water pollution has widespread health impacts, particularly in developing nations, where regulatory enforcement and treatment infrastructure are often inadequate. Contaminants not only harm humans and animals directly but also enter the food chain, with effects that can persist for decades. While some consequences appear immediately, others may remain undetected for years [30].

Unsafe water supplies contribute to approximately 4 billion cases of diarrhea annually, causing 2.2 million deaths worldwide. Poor sanitation practices—such as inadequate sewerage systems and open defecation, prevalent in regions such as sub-Saharan Africa and India—pose severe risks to water quality. According to the WHO, nearly 10 percent of the global population, or 768 million people, lack access to improved water sources, while one-third, or 2.5 billion people, lack adequate sanitation [31].

Water pollution is not confined to developing nations. For example, significant contamination has been documented in Japanese water supplies. Globally, high pollution levels have rendered substantial portions of water resources unsuitable for essential activities such as fishing, swimming, and even basic recreation.

Soil Pollution

Similar to air and water pollution, soil pollution is a significant environmental hazard. It is defined as the introduction of harmful substances into the soil, which degrade its quality and reduce its capacity to support

Figure 10.3 Most of the world's E-waste is exported to Africa, India, and China

life. Soil pollutants vary widely, encompassing natural minerals, organic and inorganic chemicals, and microorganisms. The sources of contamination are equally diverse, including solid waste, electronic waste (E-waste), nitrogen compounds, heavy metals, radioactive materials, acidic or alkaline substances, explosives, military residues, herbicides, pesticides, hydrocarbons, perchlorate, medical waste, nonrecyclable materials, and nanoparticles [32].

Solid waste is a major contributor to soil contamination and may include plastics, textiles, glass, metals, organic matter, sewage, sewage sludge, construction debris, and discarded electronics. Plastic bags, in particular, are largely nonbiodegradable and persist in soils worldwide, creating long-term environmental hazards [33] (Figure 10.3).

Industrial activities also play a significant role by producing fly ash, chemical residues, and metallic or nuclear wastes that infiltrate the soil over time. Agricultural practices are another significant source of contamination, given the extensive use of chemical fertilizers and pesticides. Pesticides, being toxic substances, not only degrade soil health but also pose direct risks to humans, animals, and plants [32].

Land Degradation

Land degradation refers to the process by which the natural productivity and ecological function of land are diminished, primarily due to human activities. It can take multiple forms, including deforestation, desertification (the clearance of vegetative cover), salinization, soil exhaustion, soil erosion, nutrient depletion, and the loss of carbon or water reserves [33].

While both natural processes and human activities can damage land, accelerated land degradation is primarily the result of anthropogenic factors (Figure 10.4).

Excessive cultivation, for example, often leads to nutrient depletion in soils, leaving them impoverished or exhausted. Without natural or artificial replenishment, soil fertility declines significantly. Salinization—the accumulation of salts in the soil—is another major cause of productivity loss, often arising from poorly managed irrigation systems. This problem is pervasive in Asia, where salinization has rendered approximately 267 million hectares of arable land unproductive, with similar impacts observed in Africa and South America.

Soil erosion, caused by unsustainable agricultural practices, overgrazing, deforestation, and natural forces such as rain and wind, further depletes soil nutrients [34]. Overgrazing by domestic livestock can remove protective grass cover, leaving soil vulnerable to erosion. Over time, this can lead to the permanent loss of vegetation cover and eventual desertification. In some cases, flooding can cause sedimentation, burying fertile soils under less productive deposits.

The scale of land degradation is global and severe. More than 20 percent of cultivated areas, 30 percent of forests, and 10 percent of grasslands worldwide have been degraded, affecting the livelihoods of

Figure 10.4 Land degradation reduces the natural productivity and ecological function of the land

Source: [36].

approximately 1.5 billion people. Over the last 50 years, land degradation has impacted half of the world's agricultural land [35]. In Latin America and the Caribbean, about 75 percent of drylands are currently affected by desertification or other forms of land degradation.

Bioaccumulation and Biomagnification

Toxic substances such as arsenic, cadmium, mercury, lead, and selenium, when discharged into freshwater ecosystems, can enter the bodies of living organisms—including plankton, benthic invertebrates, plants, birds, fish, and mammals—through a process known as bioaccumulation. Bioaccumulation is a natural physiological process that enables animals and plants to absorb and store essential substances such as vitamins, trace elements, fats, and amino acids. However, environmental pollution introduces toxic materials that can also accumulate in organisms over time, often reaching harmful levels.

A specific form of bioaccumulation is biomagnification (or amplification), which refers to the progressive increase in contaminant concentrations as they move through a food web from prey to predator [37]. In this process, the highest contaminant levels are typically found in organisms at the top of the food chain—including humans [38]. Biomagnification can be regarded as a form of secondary poisoning in ecological systems.

Bioaccumulation is facilitated by the fact that many pollutants are more soluble in lipids (fats) than in water. As a result, aquatic organisms such as phytoplankton and fish—especially species that filter large volumes of water through their gills—are prone to higher pollutant concentrations. Bioaccumulation arises from two related processes: bioconcentration (direct uptake of substances from the surrounding medium, such as water, through skin, gills, or lungs) and biomagnification (dietary uptake of contaminated prey).

As contaminants move up the food chain, higher-level consumers such as zooplankton, predatory fish (e.g., lake trout, striped bass), birds, reptiles, mammals (e.g., bears, seals), and ultimately humans, accumulate greater concentrations of pollutants. These substances can cause severe damage to the immune and reproductive systems of organisms, and some can be transferred to offspring, leading to developmental abnormalities, reproductive dysfunctions, behavioral impairments, and certain cancers.

Notable high-risk contaminants include organochlorine pesticides such as DDT (dichlorodiphenyltrichloroethane), chlordane, and toxaphene; dioxins; brominated flame retardants; heavy metal compounds; methyl mercury; and tributyltin [39].

Biosphere Deterioration

Humans are an integral part of the biosphere, and their activities both affect and are influenced by it. Virtually all socioeconomic activities bring about significant changes in the biosphere, including habitat destruction, habitat fragmentation, corridor restrictions, aquatic habitat damage, ecological disequilibrium, biodiversity loss, species extinction, deforestation, and the introduction of invasive species [40].

For example, land-consuming activities such as road building and housing development lead to the loss of natural habitats for both flora and fauna [41]. Habitat fragmentation often results from urban or industrial projects that physically or ecologically divide ecosystems, impairing their integrity. Similarly, human infrastructure and land use can block or restrict wildlife corridors—routes used by animals for daily or seasonal migration—disrupting their natural movement patterns [41].

Aquatic habitats are also vulnerable to human-induced damage. Erosion from poorly managed construction sites can destroy fish spawning beds. At the same time, alterations to flood cycles, tidal flows, and water levels may disrupt trophic dynamics, affecting the life cycles of plankton and other aquatic organisms [42].

Ecological disequilibrium occurs when non-native plant or animal species are introduced into an ecosystem, disrupting its natural balance and often harming native species. Invasive species may thrive in new environments due to the absence of natural predators or controls, sometimes spreading to dominate entire ecosystems [42].

Biodiversity loss represents one of the most serious consequences of biosphere deterioration. It is primarily driven by human activities, particularly agriculture and food production, industrialization, urbanization, road construction, tourism, and aviation.

Food Pollution

Environmental pollution can lead to both biological and chemical contamination of food. Biological contamination involves harmful microorganisms and their toxins, including aflatoxins, Salmonella, Staphylococcus, and Listeria. These pathogens can proliferate in various types of waste and significantly contaminate food products. High-protein foods such as meat and dairy are particularly vulnerable to bacterial contamination due to their nutrient-rich composition.

Chemical contamination arises from pollutants that are manufactured and subsequently released into the environment—particularly into the air and water [43]. In the United States alone, approximately 70,000 different chemicals are commercially produced [44]. Many of these chemicals enter the food chain as a result of agricultural practices, mining, transportation, and industrial manufacturing [43]. Chemical contamination of food can occur in two primary forms.

Long-term, low-level contamination from the gradual diffusion of persistent pollutants through the environment.

Short-term, high-level contamination from industrial accidents, unsafe waste disposal, or other acute pollution events.

The sources of food contamination are varied. Fertilizers such as manure and sewage sludge can contain a mix of biological and chemical contaminants. Notable chemical pollutants in food include toxic metals such as lead, cadmium, mercury, and arsenic; as well as polycyclic aromatic hydrocarbons (PAHs), polychlorinated compounds, halogenated hydrocarbon pesticides, polychlorinated biphenyls (PCBs), dioxins, polybrominated organic compounds, phthalates, and nitrites [45].

These toxic substances can bioaccumulate in aquatic organisms such as plankton, mollusks, and shellfish, with concentrations increasing through the food chain. Certain staple foods, including rice and potatoes, are particularly susceptible to contamination by mercury, lead, and arsenic. Highly carcinogenic PAHs are produced by the combustion of organic matter. They can be found in a wide range of foods due to thermal processing methods such as grilling, roasting, baking, frying, and various industrial food-processing procedures [46].

Halogenated hydrocarbon pesticides and insecticides are present globally, and because they degrade very slowly, they can contaminate food products indirectly through aquatic invertebrates, fish, birds, and mammals. In addition to biological and chemical contaminants, food may also be polluted by radiation from natural sources, nuclear reactors, processing facilities, and nuclear weapons testing.

Food Deterioration

Food deterioration can be an unintended consequence of advancements in synthetic biology. This field combines techniques from biology, genetics, chemistry, engineering, and computer science to design and construct functional biological systems. Synthetic biology operates through two main approaches: a top-down method, which modifies existing organisms, genes, and enzymes within biological material, and a bottom-up method, which creates entirely novel biochemical systems [47].

While synthetic biology can be applied to diverse sectors—including pharmaceuticals, cosmetics, and industrial materials—it plays an increasingly significant role in agriculture and food production [48]. The biological systems it produces often do not exist in nature, meaning that their modifications may have complex, long-lasting, and far-reaching effects. In food systems, such effects are especially critical, as they directly influence human health and environmental stability.

The adoption of synthetic biology in food production has accelerated over the past few decades. Genetically modified (GM) foods first entered the U.S. market in the mid-1990s. By 2000, genetically modified crops accounted for 25 percent of corn, 54 percent of soybeans, and 61 percent of cotton planted in the United States. By 2011, these figures had risen to 88 percent, 94 percent, and 90 percent, respectively [49]. Today, nearly 75 percent of processed foods in U.S. supermarkets contain GM ingredients [50].

Despite their benefits, GM foods present potential risks. Health concerns include allergic reactions, toxicity, and the development of antibiotic resistance. Environmental and ecological risks include the spread of GM traits to nontarget species, biodiversity loss, and the extinction of natural species [49]. For example, certain GM crops produce pesticides that persist in soil throughout the growing season, increasing the likelihood that insect populations will develop pesticide resistance. Furthermore, genetically modified organisms (GMOs) can displace wild species through invasiveness or genetic outcrossing.

A new generation of genetic engineering techniques is rapidly transforming the food production industry. These methods alter the genetic makeup of organisms by adding, deleting, silencing, or completely rewriting DNA [51]. Examples include genome editing tools such as CRISPR, RNA interference, metabolic engineering, and directed evolution. While these technologies hold significant promise for improving food production, their introduction into natural environments could lead to serious risks, including genetic contamination of wild species, disruption of natural ecosystems, and unforeseen health impacts.

Global Perils of Water Scarcity

Although water covers nearly 70 percent of the Earth's surface, only 2.5 percent is freshwater suitable for human use. Approximately 1.2 billion people—around 20 percent of the global population—live in areas experiencing water scarcity, while another 1.6 billion face varying levels of shortage [52]. As early as 2000, nearly one billion people lacked access to safe drinking water, and 2.5 billion lacked adequate sanitation [53]. Today, an estimated 1.8 billion people rely on water sources contaminated by fecal matter [54], contributing to roughly five million deaths annually from water-related diseases (Figure 10.5).

The crisis is worsening. Global water demand is projected to rise by 50 percent within the next two decades, surpassing the capacity of ecosystems and infrastructure to supply clean water [55]. By 2025, four billion people are expected to live under water stress, with 1.8 billion in regions of absolute scarcity [56].

The drivers of water scarcity are multifaceted, including population growth, climate change, urbanization, industrialization, shifting diets, insufficient investment, and inefficient water use. Water consumption is currently increasing at twice the rate of population growth, mainly

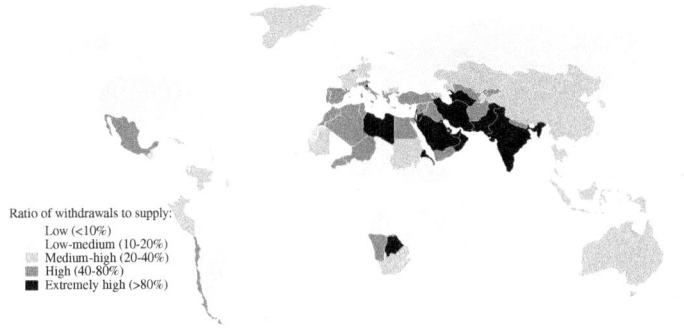

Figure 10.5 Almost 20 percent of the world's population experiences water shortage

Source: [58].

due to expanding agricultural, industrial, and public health needs [54]. Agriculture alone accounts for 70 percent of global water use, municipalities for 11 percent, and industry for 19 percent. The global population—now more than twice its size in the 1950s—is projected to exceed 8 billion by 2024, 9 billion by 2038, and 10 billion by 2056, placing unprecedented pressure on water systems.

Food production, the most water-intensive sector, accounts for more than 90 percent of total water use [55]. Dietary changes in developing countries, particularly a shift from grains to water-intensive foods such as meat and dairy, are exacerbating demand. Producing 1 kg of rice requires about 3,500 liters of water, whereas 1 kg of beef requires approximately 15,000 liters [56]. The energy sector further intensifies demand, as all forms of energy production require water across their supply chains.

Water scarcity can be classified into two main types: physical scarcity, where water supply is insufficient, and economic scarcity, where inadequate investment or poor management limits access [57]. Scarcity is often assessed by per capita water availability: regions fall under water stress when availability drops below 1,700 m^3/person/year, and under water scarcity when it falls below 1,000 m^3/person/year [52].

Some of the most water-stressed regions include the Middle East, North Africa, Central Asia, South Asia, and the Horn of Africa—areas often characterized by inequality and weak governance. The Asia-Pacific region, home to over 50 percent of the world's population, has only 36 percent of global freshwater resources. In Arab countries, per capita availability averages below 500 m³, while more than 300 million people in sub-Saharan Africa live with less than 1,000 m³ [55]. In contrast, North America and Europe enjoy much higher availability: Canada has 85,310 m³ per person, the United States 9,888 m³, and Europe averages 4,741 m³ [55].

Beyond its biological and economic functions, water is increasingly a geopolitical issue. With 60 percent of global freshwater originating from shared international river basins [56], declining availability and prolonged droughts heighten competition between states. The consequences of water scarcity extend far beyond environmental stress, posing risks of food shortages, mass migration, regional instability, economic decline, dependency on foreign aid, and even conflict over transboundary water resources.

The Drivers of Environmental Degradation

Human activity is the primary driver of environmental degradation. Factors such as overpopulation, urbanization, energy production and consumption, industrial and business activities, agriculture, and transportation, all contribute—directly or indirectly—to the deterioration of natural systems. Global population growth has been a significant force behind environmental pressures. The world's population rose sharply from 2.5 billion in 1950 to 6 billion in 2000, reaching over 8 billion in 2025. Although growth rates have slowed in some regions, population numbers will continue to rise in the coming decades, with projections indicating a global population exceeding 9 billion by 2038 [59]. Approximately 90 percent of this growth will occur in low- and middle-income countries, with sub-Saharan Africa experiencing the fastest expansion and Asia—particularly the Indian subcontinent—seeing the most significant numerical increase [15]. This rapid growth has severe implications for resource consumption, waste generation, and ecological stress.

The environmental impacts of population growth are intensified by urbanization. In 1990, only 38 percent of the world's population lived in urban areas; by 2015, the share had surpassed 50 percent. Urban populations continue to grow rapidly, and by 2050, an estimated 67 percent of the global population will reside in cities. Most of this growth will occur in developing countries, particularly in megacities across Southern and Eastern Asia [15]. Rapid urban expansion contributes to land degradation, habitat destruction and fragmentation, water pollution, GHG emissions, and air pollution. Building and demolition activities in urban centers generate significant debris and consume between one-third and one-half of the world's commodity resources. These impacts are particularly pronounced in developing nations, where high birth rates coincide with rapid urban growth.

Manufacturing remains a significant component of global economic production, especially in emerging economies, accounting for about 40 percent of world output. This sector is resource-intensive, consuming vast quantities of raw materials and energy while producing substantial solid and gaseous waste. Resource extraction has expanded dramatically—from 40 billion tons in 1980 to 58 billion tons in 2005, and 80 billion tons in 2020 [60]. This surge is driven by rising demand for base and precious metals, biomass, timber, and other materials.

Agriculture and fishing are also major contributors to environmental degradation. Global demand for food continues to rise, fueled by both population growth and changing consumption patterns. As incomes increase in emerging economies, diets shift toward higher-protein and meat-based foods, intensifying pressure on agricultural systems. The livestock sector, one of the fastest-growing components of agriculture, is projected to drive a roughly 50 percent increase in agricultural production between 2005 and 2030 [56].

The energy and transportation sectors are further key drivers of environmental decline due to their significant GHG emissions and pollutant output. Global primary energy consumption is projected to grow by 1.8 percent annually [15]. While renewable sources such as solar and wind have gained prominence, fossil fuels and nuclear energy remain dominant. Fossil fuels are expected to maintain an 85 percent share of global energy consumption until at least 2030, with only a modest decline to about 80 percent by 2050 [60].

The Consequences of Environmental Degradation

Environmental degradation has far-reaching impacts on human health, poverty, economic stability, social cohesion, and biodiversity. Its consequences are interconnected, often reinforcing one another and deepening existing vulnerabilities.

One of the most direct effects is on human health. Air and water pollution, land degradation, and GHG emissions all undermine human well-being. Water pollution alone is responsible for more than two million deaths annually worldwide, while poor air quality accounts for over 6.5million deaths each year, alongside millions of cases of respiratory illnesses such as pneumonia and asthma [10]. The release of CFCs and hydrochlorofluorocarbons (HCFCs) into the atmosphere contributes to ozone layer depletion, increasing human exposure to harmful UV radiation. Chemical and bacterial pollutants also enter food chains, contaminating fish, meat, poultry, vegetables, fruits, and grains. Industrial, agricultural, and transportation-related toxic wastes contribute to widespread disease and mortality. Land degradation processes such as desertification, deforestation, and salinization exacerbate these threats by stripping away protective natural cover, intensifying ozone depletion, and raising the risks of skin cancer and eye disease.

Poverty is another inevitable consequence. In many developing countries, poverty is closely tied to soil erosion, desertification, water scarcity, and climate variability, all of which reduce crop yields and disrupt livelihoods [23]. Declines in agricultural productivity lead to food insecurity, heightened risks of flooding and droughts, and, in extreme cases, famine. Environmental degradation in resource-scarce regions can also fuel conflict and social unrest. Economically, its impact is profound: the cost to the global economy from lost productivity, damage to infrastructure, and other impacts is estimated to reach up to 20 percent of global GDP annually [23].

Climate change and rising sea levels further compound these challenges. Coastal zones—home to about one-fifth of the world's population—are highly vulnerable, with large cities, ports, industries, and transport systems at risk of inundation. Small island states in the Indian Ocean, Caribbean, and Pacific face existential threats from submersion.

In Africa, Asia, and South America—regions with limited adaptive capacity—these risks are particularly severe. Even some areas in developed countries, including parts of Western Europe and North America, will face significant impacts. Rising seas may also provoke territorial disputes over land and maritime boundaries, while polar region changes could trigger geopolitical competition for newly accessible resources.

Resource scarcity and migration are closely linked outcomes. Water scarcity, pollution, and desertification force millions to migrate domestically or across borders. The United Nations projects that environmental migrants will number in the millions [61]. Most will originate from poor, high-birth-rate regions in Asia, South America, Africa, and the Middle East, while wealthier regions such as Europe, North America, and Australia are more likely to be destinations.

Governance challenges intensify as environmental pressures mount. Governments in highly affected countries often struggle to provide essential services, fueling frustration and political instability. Climate impacts could widen the divide between developed and developing countries, heightening tensions in international negotiations [61].

Environmental degradation also drives biodiversity loss. The destruction of habitats and shifts in climate have already caused irreversible changes to ecosystems. A World Bank study found that 15 of the planet's 24 major ecosystems were degraded [15]. Rising temperatures alone pose a critical threat: a 1°C increase could eliminate 10 percent of terrestrial species, while a 4°C rise could cause the loss of up to 30 percent [15]. Such biodiversity loss undermines ecosystem services essential for human survival, from food production to climate regulation.

The impacts are unevenly distributed, with poor and developing countries bearing the brunt. These nations, often located in tropical and subtropical regions, depend heavily on climate-sensitive sectors such as agriculture and fisheries. Limited adaptive capacity makes them especially vulnerable. Africa, for instance, could lose between 2 and 7 percent of its GDP due to increased droughts, floods, and pest outbreaks. In North Africa and the Sahel, drought, water scarcity, soil erosion, and loss of arable land are escalating problems. Egypt's Nile Delta faces threats from sea-level rise, salinization, and erosion, jeopardizing millions of livelihoods. In the Horn of Africa, Darfur, and Southern Africa, climate change, soil erosion, and food shortages have already contributed to ethnic tensions and armed conflict [61].

The Middle East is also highly exposed, with frequent droughts, reduced rainfall, sandstorms, air pollution, land degradation, and rising temperatures. Around two-thirds of Arab countries rely on external water sources [61]. Disputes over water access already exist among Jordan, Israel, Palestine, Turkey, Iraq, and Syria, and declining freshwater availability could further destabilize the region.

South Asia faces acute risks from sea-level rise. With over 40 percent of its population—nearly two billion people—living within 60 km of the coast [61], rising seas threaten both lives and infrastructure. Many of these populations remain poor and dependent on traditional agriculture, making them highly sensitive to declines in water quality, soil health, and crop yields.

Central Asia also faces environmental stress. Landlocked nations such as Kyrgyzstan and Tajikistan rely heavily on limited water resources for agriculture. Declining rainfall, water scarcity, and soil erosion are already reducing productivity.

Latin America and the Caribbean are not exempt. Coastal regions are at risk from sea-level rise, while declining rainfall and melting glaciers threaten water supplies for human use, agriculture, and energy production. These changes undermine food security and local economies.

In sum, environmental degradation undermines health, food security, economic stability, and political order while eroding the planet's biodiversity. Without urgent and coordinated action, its consequences will intensify—disproportionately affecting the most vulnerable regions and populations.

References

[1] Managi, S., ed. 2015. *The Routledge Handbook of Environmental Economics in Asia*. New York: Routledge.

[2] Yeganeh, K.H. 2020. "A Typology of Sources, Manifestations, and Implications of Environmental Degradation." *Management of Environmental Quality: An International Journal* 31, no. 3, pp. 765–783.

[3] Park, C.C. 1980. *Ecology & Environment Management*, p. 28. London: Butterworths.

[4] Dunlap, R.E., and R.J. Brulle, eds. 2015. *Climate Change and Society: Sociological Perspectives*. Oxford University Press.

[5] Babiak, K., and S. Trendafilova. 2011. "CSR and Environmental Responsibility: Motives and Pressures to Adopt Green Management Practices." *Corporate Social Responsibility and Environmental Management* 18, no. 1, pp. 11–24.

[6] Donohoe, M. 2003. "Causes and Health Consequences of Environmental Degradation and Social Injustice." *Social Science & Medicine* 56, no. 3, pp. 573–587.

[7] Menon, S., J. Hansen, L. Nazarenko, and Y. Luo. 2002. "Climate Effects of Black Carbon Aerosols in China and India." *Science* 297, no. 5590, pp. 2250–2253.

8. Mannucci, P., and M. Franchini. 2017. "Health Effects of Ambient Air Pollution in Developing Countries." *International Journal of Environmental Research and Public Health*, 14, no. 9, p. 1048.

[9] The World Health Organization. 2016. https://www.who.int/news-room/detail/12-05-2016-air-pollution-levels-rising-in-many-of-the-world-s-poorest-cities.

[10] World Energy Outlook Special Report 2016. Energy and Air Pollution. Available at https://iea.org/publications/freepublications/publication/weo-2016-special-report-energy-and-air-pollution.html.

[11] Riahi, K., D.P. Van Vuuren, E. Kriegler, J. Edmonds, B.C. O'neill, S. Fujimori, ... and W. Lutz. 2017. "The Shared Socioeconomic Pathways and Their Energy, Land Use, and Greenhouse Gas Emissions Implications: An Overview." *Global Environmental Change* 42, pp. 153–168.

[12] United States Environmental Protection Agency. 2023. "Inventory of US Greenhouse Gas Emissions and Sinks: 1990–2021 (EPA 430-R-23-002)." *US Environmental Protection Agency*. https://www.epa.gov/ghgemissions/inventory-us-greenhouse-gas-emissions-and-sinks.

[13] Melillo, J.M. 2014. *Climate Change Impacts in the United States: Highlights: US National Climate Assessment*. Government Printing Office.

[14] United Nations Environment Programme (UNEP). 2013. *Global Environment Outlook 2000*, Vol. 1. Routledge.

[15] Ruta, G. 2010. "Monitoring Environmental Sustainability Trends, Challenges, and the Way Forward." The World Bank Group.

[16] https://ourworldindata.org/grapher/ghg-emissions-by-world-region

[17] Jones et al. 2024 – with major processing by Our World in Data. Annual greenhouse gas emissions, including land use [Dataset]. Jones et al., National contributions to climate change 2024.2 [Original data]. Retrieved August 22, 2025, from the archived URL (archived on July 14, 2025).

[18] Ryghaug, M., K. Holtan Sørensen, and R. Næss. 2011. "Making Sense of Global Warming: Norwegians Appropriating Knowledge of Anthropogenic Climate Change." *Public Understanding of Science* 20, no. 6, pp. 778–795.

[19] Kampa, M., and E. Castanas. 2008. "Human Health Effects of Air Pollution." *Environmental Pollution* 151, no. 2, pp. 362–367

[20] GISTEMP Team. 2016. GISS surface temperature analysis (GISTEMP). NASA Goddard Institute for Space Studies. Dataset accessed, February 05, 2019.

[21] Harris, J.M., and B. Roach. 2007. *The Economics of Global Climate Change.* Global Development and Environment Institute, Tufts University.

[22] Solomon, S., D. Qin, M. Manning, K. Averyt, and M. Marquis, eds. 2007. *Climate Change 2007-the Physical Science Basis: Working Group I Contribution to the FOURTH ASSESsment Report of the IPCC,* Vol. 4. Cambridge University Press.

[23] Holden, E., K. Linnerud, and D. Banister. 2014. "Sustainable Development: Our Common Future Revisited." *Global Environmental Change,* 26, pp. 130–139.

[24] Morrisette, P.M. 1989. "The Evolution of Policy Responses to Stratospheric Ozone Depletion." *The Nature Resources Journal* 29, p. 793.

[25] Granier, C., and G. Brasseur. 1991. "Ozone and Other Trace Gases in the Arctic and Antarctic Regions: Three-Dimensional Model Simulations." *Journal of Geophysical Research: Atmospheres* 96, no. D2, pp. 2995–3011.

[26] Norval, M., R.M. Lucas, A.P. Cullen, F.R. De Gruijl, J. Longstreth, Y. Takizawa, and J.C. Van Der Leun. 2011. "The Human Health Effects of Ozone Depletion and Interactions with Climate Change." *Photochemical & Photobiological Sciences* 10, no. 2, pp. 199–225.

[27] Voulvoulis, N., and K. Georges. 2016. "Industrial and Agricultural Sources and Pathways of Aquatic Pollution." In *Impact of Water Pollution on Human Health and Environmental Sustainability,* pp. 29–54. IGI Global.

[28] Van Beusekom, J.E. 2018. "Eutrophication." In *Handbook on Marine Environment Protection,* pp. 429–445. Springer, Cham.

[29] UN-Water. 2014. "Water for Life 2005–2015: Water Scarcity." www .un.org/ waterforlifedecade/scarcity.shtml (accessed February 12, 2020).

[30] Ashraf, M.A., M.J. Maah, I. Yusoff, and K. Mehmood. 2010. "Effects of Polluted Water Irrigation on the Environment and Health of People in Jamber, District Kasur, Pakistan." *International Journal of Basic & Applied Sciences* 10, no. 3, pp. 37–57.

[31] WHO/UNICEF. 2013. Progress on Sanitation and Drinking-Water, 2013. Update: Joint Monitoring Programme for Water Supply and Sanitation.

[32] Tarasov, D.A., A.N. Medvedev, A.P. Sergeev, A.V. Shichkin, and A.G. Buevich. July 2017. "A Hybrid Method for the Assessment of Soil Pollutants' Spatial Distribution." *AIP Conference Proceedings* 1863, no. 1, p. 050015.

[33] Xanthos, D., and T.R. Walker. 2017. "International Policies to Reduce Plastic Marine Pollution from Single-Use Plastics (Plastic Bags and Microbeads): A Review." *Marine Pollution Bulletin* 118, no. 1–2, pp. 17–26.

[34] Lal, R. 2017. "Soil erosion by Wind and Water: Problems and Prospects." In *Soil Erosion Research Methods*, pp. 1–10. Routledge.

[35] Bossio, D., A. Noble, J. Pretty, and F. Penning de Vries. 2004. "Reversing Land and Water Degradation: Trends and "Bright Spot" opportunities." In *The Stockholm International Water Institute/Comprehensive Assessment on Water Management in Agriculture Seminar*. Stockholm.

[36] https://2021-2025.state.gov/dipnote-u-s-department-of-state-official-blog/science-speaks-land-degradation/

[37] Clayden, M.G., L.M. Arsenault, K.A. Kidd, N.J. O'Driscoll, and M.L. Mallory. 2015. "Mercury Bioaccumulation and Biomagnification in a Small Arctic Polynya Ecosystem." *Science of the Total Environment* 509, pp. 206–215.

[38] Van der Oost, R., J. Beyer, and N.P. Vermeulen. 2003. "Fish Bioaccumulation and Biomarkers in Environmental Risk Assessment: A Review." *Environmental Toxicology and Pharmacology* 13, no. 2, pp. 57–149.

[39] Galal, T. M., and H.S. Shehata. 2015. "Bioaccumulation and Translocation of Heavy Metals by Plantago Major L. grown in Contaminated Soils Under the Effect of Traffic Pollution." *Ecological Indicators* 48, pp. 244–251.

[40] Moraes, M.A.F.D., F.C.R. Oliveira, and R.A. Diaz-Chavez. 2015. "Socioeconomic Impacts of the Brazilian Sugarcane Industry." *Environmental Development* 16, pp. 31–43.

[41] Kabisch, N., S. Qureshi, and D. Haase. 2015. "Human–Environment Interactions in Urban Green Spaces—A Systematic Review of Contemporary Issues and Prospects for Future Research." Environmental Impact Assessment Review, 50, pp. 25–34.

[42] Hunter, P. 2007. "The Human Impact on Biological Diversity: How Species Adapt to Urban Challenges Sheds Light on Evolution and Provides Clues about Conservation." *EMBO Reports* 8, no. 4, pp. 316–318.

[43] Carvalho, F.P. 2017. "Pesticides, Environment, and Food Safety." *Food and Energy Security* 6, no. 2, pp. 48–60.

[44] Emerson, D. 2002. "Minnesota Exposed-From Asbestos in Back Yards to Arsenic in Wells, Environmental Contaminants Threaten the Health of Minnesotans." *Minnesota Medicine* 85, no. 10, pp. 24–32. FAO, AQUASTAT, at www.fao.org/nr/water/aquastat/water_use/index.stm.

[45] Túri-Szerletics, M., and I. Patkó. 2008. "Environmental Contaminants in Foodstuffs." *Acta Polytechnica Hungarica* 5, no. 3, pp. 135–140.

[46] Caballero, B., L.C. Truco, and P. Finglas. 2003. *Encyclopedia of Food Science and Nutrition*. 2nd ed., pp. 1595–1598, 3051–3055, 3508–3509, 4617–4619, p. 4136. UK: Elsevier Science Ltd., Academic Press.

[47] Gaiteri, C., M. Chen, B. Szymanski, K. Kuzmin, J. Xie, C. Lee, T. Blanche, E. Chaibub Neto, S.-C. Huang, T. Grabowski, T. Madhyastha, and V. Komashko. 2015. "Identifying Robust Communities and Multi-Community Nodes by Combining Top-Down and Bottom-Up Approaches to Clustering." *Scientific Reports* 5, p. 16361.

[48] Moses, T., and A. Goossens. 2017. "Plants for Human Health: Greening Biotechnology and Synthetic Biology." *Journal of Experimental Botany* 68, no. 15, p. 4009.

[49] Homer, M.B. 2011. "Frankenfish-It is What is for Dinner: The FDA, Genetically Engineered Salmon, and the Flawed Regulation of Biotechnology." *Columbia Journal of Law and Social Problems* 45, p. 83.

[50] Young, S. 2010. "Safety of Genetically Modified Salmon Debated." *CNN*, http://www.cnn.com/2010/ HEALTH/09/20/genetically.engineered.salmon/ index.html.

[51] Balmer, A., and P. Martin. 2008. *Synthetic Biology. Social and Ethical Challenges.*

[52] World Water Assessment Programme (WWAP). 2012. *World Water Development Report, Vol. 1: Managing Water Under Uncertainty and Risk.* Paris: UNESCO.

[53] Schlosser, C.A., K. Strzepek, X. Gao, C. Fant, E. Blanc, S. Paltsev, and A. Gueneau. 2014. "The Future of Global Water Stress: An Integrated Assessment." *Earth's Future* 2, no. 8, pp. 341–361.

[54] UN-Water. 2006. Coping with Water Scarcity: Strategic Issue and Priority for System-wide Action. *UN-Water Thematic Initiatives.*

[55] *Water under Uncertainty and Risk.* 2012. Paris: UNESCO.

[56] FAO, AQUASTAT. 2013. Available at fao.org/nr/water/aquastat/water _use/index.stm (accessed March 01, 2020).

[57] U.N. Food and Agriculture Organization (FAO). 2012. *Coping with Water Scarcity: An Action Framework for Agriculture and Food Security.* FAO Water Report 38, Rome.

[58] Kummu, M., J.H. Guillaume, H. De Moel, S. Eisner, M. Flörke, M. Porkka, ... and P.J. Ward. 2016. "The World's Road to Water Scarcity: Shortage and Stress in the 20th Century and Pathways Towards Sustainability." *Scientific Reports* 6, no.1, p. 38495.

[59] Bloom, D.E. 2011. "7 Billion and Counting." *Science* 333, no. 6042, pp. 562–69.

[60] OECD. 2008. *OECD Environmental Outlook to 2030.* Organisation for Economic Co-Operation and Development, Paris.

[61] Mann, M.E. 2009. "Do Global Warming and Climate Change Represent a Serious Threat to Our Welfare and Environment?" *Social Philosophy and Policy* 26, no. 2, pp. 193–230.

Index

Note: Page numbers followed by "f" refers to figures and "t" refers to tables.

www.ingramcontent.com/pod-product-compliance
Lightning Source LLC
Chambersburg PA
CBHW061506180526

45171CB00001B/62

9 781637 429341